Around the Table with Jesus

Around the Table with Jesus

Lori Beth Wagner

A Bible Study & Devotional for Lent with Mediterranean Recipes

invite PRESS

Plano, Texas

Around the Table with Jesus:
A Bible Study and Devotional for Lent with Mediterranean Recipes

Copyright 2025 by Lori Beth Wagner

This book is printed on acid-free, elemental chlorine-free paper.

Paperback 978-1-96326-540-8; ePub 978-1-96326-541-5

25 26 27 28 29 30 31 32 33 34—10 9 8 7 6 5 4 3 2 1

MANUFACTURED in the UNITED STATES of AMERICA

Contents

A Seven-Week Bible Study with Recipes

My Lenten Journal

Preface

Lent is a time when we usually think of fasting, but Jesus spent most of his time feasting! This series of meditations and their accompanying seven-week Bible study can be used individually or communally around the table with Jesus as he journeys his way to the cross.

In the Jewish tradition, story sharing around food binds families and friends together in a common history and identity. The sharing of food for Christians too can be not only a time of community and bonding, but a sacred time and space in which the presence of the Holy Spirit of Christ sits as head of our table, blessing and healing all who join him. When Jesus joined with his disciples in his "last supper," he invited them to remember him and honor him every time they gathered for a meal together. This study provides an opportunity for you as disciples to gather together with Jesus as he journeys through the last weeks of his life on earth.

Within these pages, you'll find a Bible Study, a Lenten Devotional, space for your own Lenten Journal, and a Planning Calendar for using this resource. This study is meant to accompany prepared meals. You may want to start by assigning different groups to specific weeks for preparing and serving food. You may also want to decide ahead of time which parts of the study you'll do together before, during, and after the meal. Each week, the group preparing the meal should elect a leader who will guide the rest of the group through the questions and activities that accompany the meal and the study.

The Bible study begins on Ash Wednesday and is designed to run seven weeks with an optional eighth session, ending just after Easter Sunday with a Resurrection Feast. The study uses some of the content and flavor of the daily meditations but adds prayers and discussion questions that are designed to provoke deeper thought into Jesus' last days, and deeper faith, as you enter into conversation with him in his own time and culture.

Both the study and the devotionals are deeply personal and relational and are centered around meals that echo the metaphors and moods of your own Lenten journey. These meals use Mediterranean foods consistent with Jesus' time, yet they are easy to prepare. They are healthy (think *salve*) recipes that allow our daily "bread" to be energy for the body, food for thought, and loving nurture for the soul.

As you gather in preparation and feasting together, allow the food as well as the conversation to deepen your relationships with Jesus and with each other. Make your table time a time for honest sharing! May your journey be blessed!

How to Use These Resources

You can use these resources in two or three ways:

1. You can use the seven-week Bible study alone as a gathering time and Lenten mealtime. I recommend gathering an hour or two before the study for those preparing the recipes. Then meet for the study, which encompasses seven (optionally eight) meal recipes along with prayers, readings, discussion questions and activities, a Lenten challenge, and a designated meal.

2. Alternatively, or in conjunction with the study, you can use the devotional part of the material in three ways:

    a. A twenty-four-day journey (starting March 30) of daily meal devotionals with breakfast, lunch, and dinner devotionals, as well as personal menus for you and your family. Because of the intensive nature of this journey, this has been created as a twenty-four-day devotional. Read each devotional as you partake of the suggested meals for each day. This journey encompasses an entire Lenten journey within half of the time (twenty-four days).

b. You can also opt to do the forty-eight-day Lenten devotional journey. Because of the intensity, this devotional suggests expanding the journey to encompass the entire Lenten experience from Ash Wednesday through Easter Monday. On Day One, for example, you would serve breakfast as "brunch" and lunch as "dinner." On Day Two you would repeat the same "brunch" (breakfast) but use the "Dinner" menu for dinner. In other words, each day is split into two parts, so as to double the resurrection journey to fill the entire Lenten calendar. This slightly lighter fare may still be plenty of food for the average Lenten pilgrim and may allow more preparation time each day for that special devotional time with Jesus.

c. You can do the twenty-four-day journey but do it every other day, leaving more time for reflection and having some downtime in between, or time for eating the leftovers! If you choose this option, you may want to do some private reflection or spend some of your own time with Jesus on the days in between.

Of course, the ultimate "feast" is to attend the weekly Bible study, as well as reading through the daily devotional meditations, which will directly follow Jesus' heart-wrenching story from Capernaum to the Cave of Resurrection!

I hope your journey is sumptuous, fulfilling, nourishing, and refreshing. Mazel tov!

A Seven-Week
Bible Study
with Recipes

Feasting with Jesus on His Journey to the Cross

Menu: *Tilapia Capernaum, Roasted Mediterranean Vegetables, Red Wine or Grape Juice*

Recipe: *Cut tomatoes, broccoli, zucchini, onion, and eggplant or potatoes into slices. Toss them with salt, pepper, and olive oil. Season with Sebah Baharat (a mix of Mediterranean spices) or with anise seed. Prepare Tilapia on baking sheet. Create rub with pinch of ginger, cilantro, turmeric, and black pepper. Rub on fish. Then drizzle with olive oil and line with olives, lemon, and capers. Bake 400 for 25 minutes.*

Shopping List: *tomatoes, broccoli, zucchini, onion, eggplant or potatoes, olive oil, Mediterranean spice or anise seed, tilapia, ginger, cilantro, turmeric, black pepper, lemon, wine or grape juice.*

Prayer

Lord Jesus, every day we spend with you is a feast of blessing. Let us join you now at your table. For you are the host of this and every gathering. As your loyal disciples, we look forward to this time with you—your presence, your teaching, your nourishment, and your wisdom. May we break bread together in the knowledge and blessing of your powerful presence. Amen.

Backdrop/Geographical Portrait

Early in Jesus' ministry, he moved his residence from Nazareth to Capernaum, a multi-cultural seaport on the northwestern coast of the Sea of Galilee. Known for its olives and olive presses, industrial Capernaum stood prominently along the famous "Via Maris" trade route, called in the Scriptures the "Way of the Sea." There Jesus would encounter people from all walks of life, cultures, and regions. Jesus taught devout Jews in the local synagogue in Capernaum, but he also gathered interested followers from all over the known world, as they encountered him ministering and healing in town, by the port, and beside the sea. As his name grew, they began to look for him whenever they came to port.

Import taxes were an important source of income for the Roman government in cities such as Capernaum. Along the port of Capernaum, Roman-Jewish tax collectors stood in booths, making sure all incoming food and wares were properly taxed and payments recorded. Here Jesus would meet Levi, later known as Matthew, a worldly and educated man, proficient in languages and mathematics, who would later become a writer of a Gospel and leader among Jesus' apostles.

As the Sea of Galilee was rich with life, the fishing industry held prominence in Capernaum Seaport. St. Peter's Fish, the local name for tilapia, is a common fish in the Sea of Galilee. It would have been eaten daily by Jesus and his disciples in Capernaum. Capernaum was also a major center for the olive processing industry. There olives were pressed for their oil and the remains used for items such as soap.

Wine was the drink of choice with meals. Red wines were made from local grapes. In this rich cultural center, our table time with Jesus begins.

Story

The Son of Man Came Eating and Drinking

"Truly I tell you, among those born of women there has not risen anyone greater than John the Baptist; yet whoever is least in the kingdom

2

of heaven is greater than he. From the days of John the Baptist until now, the kingdom of heaven has been subjected to violence, and violent people have been raiding it. For all the Prophets and the Law prophesied until John. And if you are willing to accept it, he is the Elijah who was to come. Whoever has ears, let them hear.

"To what can I compare this generation? They are like children sitting in the marketplaces and calling out to others:

'We played the pipe for you,

and you did not dance;

we sang a dirge,

and you did not mourn.'

For John came neither eating nor drinking, and they say, 'He has a demon.' The Son of Man came eating and drinking, and they say, 'Here is a glutton and a drunkard, a friend of tax collectors and sinners.' But wisdom is proved right by her deeds.

Then Jesus began to denounce the towns in which most of his miracles had been performed, because they did not repent. (Matthew 11:11–20)

Jesus Feasts with Matthew the Tax Collector and His Friends

As Jesus went on from there, he saw a man named Matthew sitting at the tax collector's booth. "Follow me," he told him, and Matthew got up and followed him.

While Jesus was having dinner at Matthew's house, many tax collectors and sinners came and ate with him and his disciples. When the Pharisees saw this, they asked his disciples, "Why does your teacher eat with tax collectors and sinners?"

On hearing this, Jesus said, "It is not the healthy who need a doctor, but the sick. But go and learn what this means: 'I desire mercy, not sacrifice.' For I have not come to call the righteous, but sinners."

Then John's disciples came and asked him, "How is it that we and the Pharisees fast often, but your disciples do not fast?"

Jesus answered, "How can the guests of the bridegroom mourn while he is with them? The time will come when the bridegroom will be taken from them; then they will fast.

"No one sews a patch of unshrunk cloth on an old garment, for the patch will pull away from the garment, making the tear worse. Neither do people pour new wine into old wineskins. If they do, the skins will burst; the wine will run out and the wineskins will be ruined. No, they pour new wine into new wineskins, and both are preserved." (Matthew 9:9–17)

Imagine

Imagine Jesus with you at this table. Raise your glass and toast to your relationship with him as his disciple, and to the walk you are preparing to take with him. Your fast is a celebration. Your meal is not the dregs of water and bread but the succulent and lavish feast of the Holy Spirit.

While you are laughing and talking with Jesus, someone taps him on the shoulder for a moment and whispers in a low voice you can hear: "What's wrong with you? Why are you and your disciples celebrating like this when everyone else is fasting?" Jesus says to them, "Imagine there's a wedding going on. Would you ignore the bridegroom's festivities and fast? Those who have never tasted something new in a new way won't know what they are missing. They'll always say, 'The old way is good enough for me!' And for some, they'll never be happy but will always find something to criticize. They criticized John for his fasting habits, and me for my feasting. Instead of worrying about what is going into our bodies, perhaps we should think more about what is coming out." The man walks away shaking his head.

Table Talk

- ❧ What are you thinking about as you witness this encounter at your table?

- ❧ What do you think Jesus means by his responses? By his actions? What is Jesus trying to teach us?

- ❧ What would you like to ask Jesus about his interaction? About his teaching? What do you hear him telling you about your own life that feels new and fresh?

- ❧ What have been the most memorable mealtimes in your life? Who was there? What did you talk about? How would having Jesus there change the conversation?

- ❧ How does your table today feel different with Jesus at the head as your host? Describe your feelings.

- ❧ What areas in your life make you feel malnourished? Why do you think you feel that way?

- ❧ What do you most hunger and thirst for in your life that you feel is sometimes unfulfilled?

- ❧ How can Jesus nourish the hungry part of you? What do you feel Jesus calling you to change about yourself or your life? How can Jesus help you do that?

- ❧ How can the food on your table blessed by the presence of Jesus feed you and sustain you through the hard times in your life?

- ❧ What do you think Jesus was feeling at this point in his journey? Why?

Roundtable Relational Activity

Gather while holding hands around the table. Take turns praying. What prayer do you need to pray that will sustain you through a journey you are experiencing in your life right now? Pray for your greatest weakness to be revealed, and Jesus' strength to fill you and fuel you, so that your weakness becomes your strength.

Lenten Challenge

Find time this week to spend with Jesus at your table in prayer. Be aware that he is there with you. What questions do you want to ask him? What do you feel him saying to you about your life and your relationships? About your faith? Record your experiences in your Lenten Journal.

Meal

Jesus tells you, "Seek out the kind of food that will be of lasting value in your life, the spiritual food that comes from the Son of Man, the One on whom God the Father has placed his own seal of blessing." Think about what that might mean to you in your own life.

While you are nourishing your body with St. Peter's Fish, nourish your spirit with prayer. Tasting food can be tangible prayer. Savor each bite slowly. Experience the various tastes within the food. What stories in Scripture about Jesus remind you of St. Peter's Fish? Share them at the table with each other.

Closing Prayer

Lord Jesus, as I begin this Lenten time around the table with you, I pray for insight, compassion, and wisdom. Thank you for the companionship of your presence, the strength of your sustenance, the simplicity of your love that can lead only to a deepening of my faith. My soul finds nourishment in you, and with you I am filled and fulfilled. Amen.

Dressing for Dinner

Menu: *Moroccan Chicken (or Lamb), Potato and Spinach Curry, Red Wine or Grape Juice*

Recipe: *In slow cooker, add boneless chicken, sautéed onions and garlic, ginger, paprika, cumin, oregano, turmeric, cinnamon, coriander, bay leaf, lemon, and olives with tomatoes and broth. Cook 5 hours. Cook spinach with garlic, ginger, and onions. Then puree. Add cumin, coriander, garam masala, cooked potatoes, and a small amount of cream or yogurt. Cook gently.*

Shopping List: *chicken, onions, garlic, herbs and spices, tomatoes, chicken broth, olives, frozen or fresh spinach, small potatoes, cream.*

Prayer

Lord, as I gather with friends and family, I thank you for coming not just into my life, but into my home. Even when I wander away, you seek me out. For this I am always grateful. I come into your presence with an open heart for seeing all things new. Amen.

Backdrop/Geographical Portrait

Jesus spent a lot of time with his friends Mary, Martha, and Lazarus in a little place called Bethany, on a hill a few miles outside of Jerusalem.

We don't know a lot about this family, but they may have been moderately wealthy—at least enough to host people frequently. It is possible that Lazarus had some connection to Jerusalem. It appears that Mary and Martha are either widows being cared for in their brother's household or single women whose father had passed away. No matter what their situation, we know that these are most likely wealthy benefactors capable of living independently as a family. As Martha is called the "Lady of the House," it is likely that their parents have passed on. It could also be that the brother and sisters were pledged to follow the ways of the Essenes, whose lives were often devoted to the care of the ill and outcast.

One theory about Bethany is that it may have been an Essene hospice of sorts for those dealing with leprosy, cancer, or other fatal diseases.

Whoever they were, Jesus was fond of them. Lazarus appears to be a close friend and supporter of Jesus' ministry. He was definitely a benefactor. Jesus sought solace in Bethany several times in his final weeks. In fact, his raising of Lazarus became a provocative event. When news spread about what he had done, a "hit" was put out not just on Jesus' head, but on Lazarus as well!

We know too that Jesus likely loved to frequent the home at Bethany for its ample food and conversation. Martha and Mary cooked and served. The disciples, along with Lazarus and other supporters who had gathered, would have reclined around the table there many times, eating and drinking, talking of the events occurring and the difficult times to come.

Story

The Story of Mary and Martha

As Jesus and his disciples were on their way, he came to a village where a woman named Martha opened her home to him. She had a sister called Mary, who sat at the Lord's feet listening to what he said. But Martha was distracted by all the preparations that had to be made.

She came to him and asked, "Lord, don't you care that my sister has left me to do the work by myself? Tell her to help me!"

"Martha, Martha," the Lord answered, "you are worried and upset about many things, but few things are needed—or indeed only one. Mary has chosen what is better, and it will not be taken away from her" (Luke 10:38–42).

Jesus' Parable of the Wedding Feast

Jesus spoke to them again in parables, saying: "The kingdom of heaven is like a king who prepared a wedding banquet for his son. He sent his servants to those who had been invited to the banquet to tell them to come, but they refused to come.

Again, he sent other servants, saying, "Tell those who are invited, 'See, I have prepared my dinner, my oxen and my fat calves have been slaughtered, and everything is ready. Come to the wedding feast.'"

"But they paid no attention and went off—one to his field, another to his business. The rest seized his servants, mistreated them and killed them. The king was enraged. He sent his army and destroyed those murderers and burned their city.

"Then he said to his servants, 'The wedding feast is ready, but those I invited did not deserve to come. So go to the street corners and invite to the banquet anyone you find.' So the servants went out into the streets and gathered all the people they could find, the bad as well as the good, and the wedding hall was filled with guests.

"But when the king came in to see the guests, he noticed a man there who was not wearing wedding clothes. He asked, 'How did you get in here without wedding clothes, friend?' The man was speechless.

"Then the king told the attendants, 'Tie him hand and foot, and throw him outside, into the darkness, where there will be weeping and gnashing of teeth.'

"For many are invited, but few are chosen" (Matthew 22:1–14).

Imagine

No matter how insignificant we think we are, or how mundane our lives may seem to be, Jesus is never too "important" to spend time with any one of us. Imagine today that you've been looking out for Jesus in your life. Imagine Jesus saying to you, "I need to come to your house today!" During lunch, imagine Jesus dining with you. He is your house guest, and this time is set aside just for the two of you to get to know each other, to talk, to eat, and to pray together. Pray with him now.

Remember the story of Mary and Martha? Both were dear to Jesus. But Martha was so concerned with details of "hospitality," with getting the food just right, with setting the table just so, with fussing over cleaning the pots, maintaining decorum, and getting things in order, that she didn't have time to sit at the table. When we get ready to go to a banquet, we so often think of bathing well, styling our hair, making sure our clothing is appropriate, and putting on our best decorum. Sometimes we can get so concerned with all of these trivialities that the "meal with friends" becomes more of a show to get through than a relaxing and relational *selah*! At the feast that Jesus prepares, he invites us not to "dress up" in our finest material things, but to "dress" ourselves within God's cloak of grace. When we put on the dressings of authenticity, openness, transparency, and intimacy, we dress in the robes of relationship and show God that we are interested not in how to "put on airs," but in the winds of the Spirit that God provides. Being "dressed" for the feast means to receive the gift of relationship, to come in gratitude and thanks to the table. For to Christ, it doesn't matter if you can afford gold or precious stones, or whether you dress in silk or burlap. God is interested only in the dressings of your heart and the sincerity of your presence. The ninth letter of the Greek alphabet is *iota* (intimacy, openness, transparency). Dressing to the "nines" for Jesus' banquet means to come wearing only an iota of your means. Like Mary, be prepared today to sit at the feet of Jesus, to revel in his grace, and to realize that his interest in you is all about *who you are* and nothing about how you cover up your faults. Unwrap the hindrances that bind you today and prepare to come to the banquet with Jesus, just as you are.

Table Talk

> ⤳ Read the Scripture about the parable Jesus tells regarding being "dressed" for dinner. How do you understand what Jesus is teaching us?

> ⤳ In what ways do you hide in your life? What kinds of "dressings" in your life cover up your ability to be authentic and true to who you are?

> ⤳ What do you think it means to be "clothed" in God's righteousness?

> ⤳ Think about wedding garb. Why do you think Jesus is so often compared to a bridegroom in Scripture? What does that say about the garments you put on?

> ⤳ What does it mean to come to the table with Jesus?

Roundtable Relational Activity

In your group, share an intimate and authentic story about yourself. Was it hard to tell your story? Why or why not? How did the group react to your story?

Pray together, holding hands around the table. Jesus is affirming and blessing you. Claim your story, because it is yours. Whether your story is difficult or light, funny or hard, how does your story inform your life? How has that experience helped form your identity?

Draw a picture of your favorite memory of table time. Who is at your table? Where are you in the picture? What is happening? Who is conversing? What do you love most about this memory?

Lenten Challenge

Think about the various "tables" in your life. Are some more authentic than others? Why do you think so? Do you feel more authentic with your table of friends or your table of family? Which tables have Jesus at the head and as the host? How might you form a new table within your community with people you don't know well?

This week, invite someone new to your table. Take the time to listen to his or her stories. Tell one of yours. How has this experience changed your relationship? Journal about your experience.

Meal

As you partake of your meal together, pay attention to the signs of Jesus' presence around you at the table. Feel his compassion, acceptance, and love. Feel his mercy among you and within you. Feel his comfort. Jesus knows you inside and out. Allow your heart to open, allowing him to see you in all of your joys and sorrows, mistakes and successes. Feel Jesus' smile upon you. Bathe in the warmth of his grace. Jesus loves you just because you are you.

Closing Prayer

Lord, allow me to be my most authentic self, to throw off the bulky worries that weigh me down, to cast off stress and doubt, and to sit at your feet, feasting on your power and grace. Help me to be filled with your love and nourished by your presence. Clothe me in your peace and love. Help me to be aware of your presence even in the midst of a world that doubts. Here in my time with you, I am renewed and refreshed, restored, and relaxed. Amen.

The Healing Power of Fish

> **Menu:** Cod Mediterranean, Rice or Couscous, Stuffed Grape Leaves, Red Wine or Grape Juice
>
> **Recipe:** Make a sauce of chopped tomatoes, tomato paste, capers, olives, and pepper, and heat it slowly in a pan. Place your fish in a casserole dish topped with bay leaf, peppercorns, lemon rind, and onions. Bake for 25 minutes. Top with the sauce, some parsley, and lemon. Prepare rice or couscous with pine nuts. Provide stuffed grape leaves.
>
> **Shopping List:** chopped tomatoes (can), tomato paste, capers, olives, cod, bay leaf, peppercorns, lemon, onions, parsley, rice or couscous, grape leaves, grape juice or wine.

Prayer

Lord Jesus, infuse me with a passionate faith. Give me the strength to persevere in my faith, even when I am challenged to reach beyond what I know. Let the Holy Spirit light up my spirit so that I might be a beacon of your hope to others. Amen.

Backdrop/Geographical Portrait

In Jesus' time, emerging fishing industries flourished along the Sea of Galilee. The town of Magdala had become a sardine pickling hub, and Capernaum had become a major trading port for many food products. It's no wonder that Jesus chose several fishermen as disciples.

Fishing during the first century was not an easy profession. It took grit, determination, patience, and endurance. Fishermen worked long hours, not only on the sea but when sitting in the heat of the day mending nets. Most net fishing took place during the night. Fishermen would set out several hundred yards from shore, drop their nets, and then hoist and drag the nets to shore with their boats, sorting out unwanted creatures and tossing the best fish into baskets to be taxed and sold.

Although fishing was a lucrative industry and many entrepreneurs, such as the fishing mogul Zebedee, had several employees working for them, it required strength and hard work, day and night. Not only did fishermen weather literal storms, but they never knew what their nets would yield from one day to the next.

Nets were all important for this kind of fishing. While individuals might fish with hooks and sinkers, fishing in bulk as an industry required large, strong nets. Nets were made of linen. Each day, the nets needed to be repaired, washed, and dried to preserve them from wear and tear. Holes were mended, debris was removed, and the pieces of stone that served as weights and sinkers on the bottom of the nets would frequently need replacing. Doing this work took strength, guts, and character, qualities Jesus valued in the unusual group of disciples he was gradually forming.

Story

Jesus Calls Fishermen as Disciples

When Jesus heard that John had been put in prison, he withdrew to Galilee. Leaving Nazareth, he went and lived in Capernaum, which was by the lake in the area of Zebulun and Naphtali—to fulfill what was said through the prophet Isaiah:

"Land of Zebulun and land of Naphtali,

the Way of the Sea, beyond the Jordan,

Galilee of the Gentiles—

the people living in darkness

have seen a great light;

on those living in the land of the shadow of death

a light has dawned."

From that time on Jesus began to preach, "Repent, for the kingdom of heaven has come near."

As Jesus was walking beside the Sea of Galilee, he saw two brothers, Simon called Peter and his brother Andrew. They were casting a net into the lake, for they were fishermen. "Come, follow me," Jesus said, "and I will send you out to fish for people." At once they left their nets and followed him.

Going on from there, he saw two other brothers, James son of Zebedee and his brother John. They were in a boat with their father Zebedee, preparing their nets. Jesus called them, and immediately they left the boat and their father and followed him.

Jesus went throughout Galilee, teaching in the synagogues, proclaiming the good news of the kingdom, and healing every disease and sickness among the people. News about him spread all over Syria, and people brought to him all who were ill with various diseases, those suffering severe pain, the demon-possessed, those having seizures, and the paralyzed; and he healed them. Large crowds from Galilee, the Decapolis, Jerusalem, Judea and the region across the Jordan followed him (Matthew 4:12–25).

Jesus Feeds with Bread and Fish, then Walks on Water, and Heals in Gennesaret

When Jesus landed and saw a large crowd, he had compassion on them and healed their sick.

As evening approached, the disciples came to him and said, "This is a remote place, and it's already getting late. Send the crowds away, so they can go to the villages and buy themselves some food."

Jesus replied, "They do not need to go away. You give them something to eat."

"We have here only five loaves of bread and two fish," they answered.

"Bring them here to me," he said. And he directed the people to sit down on the grass. Taking the five loaves and the two fish and looking up to heaven, he gave thanks and broke the loaves. Then he gave them to the disciples, and the disciples gave them to the people. They all ate and were satisfied, and the disciples picked up twelve basketfuls of broken pieces that were left over. The number of those who ate was about five thousand men, besides women and children.

Immediately Jesus made the disciples get into the boat and go on ahead of him to the other side, while he dismissed the crowd. After he had dismissed them, he went up on a mountainside by himself to pray. Later that night, he was there alone, and the boat was already a considerable distance from land, buffeted by the waves because the wind was against it.

Shortly before dawn Jesus went out to them, walking on the lake. When the disciples saw him walking on the lake, they were terrified. "It's a ghost," they said, and cried out in fear.

But Jesus immediately said to them: "Take courage! It is I. Don't be afraid."

"Lord, if it's you," Peter replied, "tell me to come to you on the water."

"Come," he said.

Then Peter got down out of the boat, walked on the water and came toward Jesus. But when he saw the wind, he was afraid and, beginning to sink, cried out, "Lord, save me!"

Immediately Jesus reached out his hand and caught him. "You of little faith," he said, "why did you doubt?"

And when they climbed into the boat, the wind died down. Then those who were in the boat worshiped him, saying, "Truly you are the Son of God."

When they had crossed over, they landed at Gennesaret. And when the men of that place recognized Jesus, they sent word to all the surrounding country. People brought all their sick to him and begged him to let the sick just touch the edge of his cloak, and all who touched it were healed (Matthew 14:14–36).

Imagine

Jesus had very good reasons for calling several fishermen to be in discipleship with him. Have you ever gone fishing? If you have, you know that whether standing knee-deep fly-fishing or sitting in a boat on the water, while enjoyable, this favorite pastime can also take a lot of patience, endurance, and time, and it can be quite challenging, even more so for a fisher who makes their living from fishing. In Jesus' day, fishermen could spend days on the sea sitting and casting their nets with nothing to show for it. They persevered through all kinds of storms, endured all kinds of hardships, tossed to and fro on little boats, and spent many a slow day with only patience and hope that they would stumble upon the right place and the right time that would yield a net full of fish. When they did, they took everything that came into the net. Sometimes they might catch some very strange creatures, other times, only some small minnows. But whatever came to them, they were thankful for, and they worked together to haul in the net. Then they went out again the next day. They didn't fear failure. They knew that in order to find that right place and right time when the fish were plentiful, they needed to be out on the sea, watching and waiting, casting and adventuring.

To be "fishers" of people takes patience too. You can't choose which fish come into the net. You take them all, and you love them all. You sail the seas, and you swim with the seafood. How do you know when you are in the right place at the right time to save a life for Jesus? How do you know when the time is ripe? You don't. But if you don't go out and sail the seas or splash among the fish, if you don't "go deep" in your discipleship journey, you will never be that saving grace for someone who really needs to come ashore. For Jesus, fishers are lifesavers, not life takers. Their rugged hands are filled with grace.

Table Talk

- Tonight, as you savor your fish, remember the people in your life who cast nets. Who taught you to pray, caught your attention, sought your life, brought you to Jesus? Who were your fishers? And for whom will you be that fisher too?

- How has your fear of failure kept you from getting to know people in your community? How has that fear kept you from listening to their fears, hopes, and questions about faith and Jesus? How has that fear kept you from listening to their stories?

- Why do you think it's important to think about the disciples' call stories near the time of Jesus' death? What does he want you to remember about fishing for your life? For your church?

- Why does Jesus spend so much time teaching in the last months of his ministry? What does he so urgently need his disciples and others to understand about his mission for the world?

- What does it mean to "go deep" when it comes to your discipleship, your relationships with God and others?

➤ What does Jesus' healing ministry reveal about his mission? About our call to discipleship?

Roundtable Relational Activity

Share with each other the story of your own faith journey. Can you remember a time in your life when someone reminded you of Jesus' love, care, and presence? How did it make you feel?

Did you keep in touch with that person? Why or why not?

Lenten Challenge

This week, ask some friends or family to tell you about a time when they felt divine presence in their lives. Listen to their stories. Write down your reflections about what you heard in your Lenten Journal.

Meal

As you prepare to share this meal together, think about the story of Christ's sacrifice and resurrection and our celebration of his salvation in our lives. Can you see yourself in Christ's story?

Closing Prayer

Lord Jesus, let my hands be your hands, my eyes be your eyes, my life be your life. Give me the heart and mind of a fisher and a soul filled with your grace. Amen.

The Stew over Bread

Menu: *Lentil Stew, Bread, Red Wine or Grape Juice*

Recipe: *In a large pot, add lentils, chicken broth, tomatoes, carrots, potatoes, celery, basil, garlic, pepper, cauliflower, chickpeas, cumin, turmeric, cinnamon, and a bay leaf. Cook 50 minutes until tender. Serve with freshly baked bread and wine or juice.*

Shopping List: *lentils, chicken broth, tomatoes, carrots, potatoes, celery, basil, garlic, pepper, cauliflower, chickpeas, cumin, turmeric, cinnamon, bread, and bay leaf. And, of course, salt.*

Prayer

Lord Jesus, help me to start today by basking in the freshness of your Spirit and the warmth of your presence. Prepare me with your love and mercy. Knead my heart with faith. Raise my life to hope. Salt my mission with love. Teach my soul to desire only you. Amen.

Backdrop/Geographical Portrait

Salt in Jesus' day was a very important ingredient, not only for seasoning but also for healing, preserving, purifying, burning, and livening things up. Salt was used in every Temple and table offering. "Season all your grain offerings with salt," says Leviticus 2:13. Whenever you shared a meal at the table, you were to use salt. For a sacrifice to be acceptable to God, it had to be salted. Therefore, as those who sacrifice their lives in discipleship to Jesus, we must be salted as well with the compassion and gratitude of our Lord's amazing sacrifice, and salted with the grace that sends us into the world to offer up living food to those in need of Jesus.

Salt can symbolize tears, like the tears that Jesus shed for Jerusalem and for the sin of humanity. When we sit down to feast with Jesus, we become part of the living sacrifice and part of the living bread that revives, flavors, and feeds others.

But there is an even more important symbol for salt. Leviticus 2:13 refers to God's covenant with humanity as a covenant of salt. It was a covenant that was incorruptible, unbreakable, passionate, and seasoned with love. Salt stood for permanence (the way meat could be preserved), as the covenant between humanity and God is permanent. Salt also purifies. Humans are by nature often lacking in spiritual purity; therefore, our sacrifice in the form of a meal taken together should be seasoned with salt, as we must ourselves be seasoned by Christ. Christ seasons within us the grace and passion that defines our lives as disciples and reveals the way we "taste" to others who encounter us.

Bread was the staple of the Mediterranean meal. Leaven created soft risen bread, while unleavened bread remained crisp and flat. Jesus would use both metaphors frequently in his teaching. Jesus is the Bread of Life, our nourishment, and our staple. When we are fed with the Bread of Jesus, we become likewise spiritual food for a hungry world. Leaven can define the way bread will behave. Jesus uses this metaphor to describe the nature of the disciples of the Kingdom of God, but also to describe the nature of the Pharisees and Sadducees. Their behaviors and motives are different. But both are driven by their own unique kind of "leaven," the inclinations that reside within our hearts. Jesus told us that it is not what goes into our mouths that defiles, but what comes out!

Things were stewing around this time in Jesus' life and missional journey. After the raising of Lazarus, news got out to the chief priests and Pharisees about what Jesus had done, and they called a council meeting to talk about what to do. Many of the people were rallying around Jesus more and more, and the authorities began to be truly afraid of what could happen next. Temple officials feared that the Romans would think they were not keeping their word to them or that they could not handle keeping the peace in Jerusalem. What if the Romans thought the people were going to revolt? What if the Romans decided it was better to destroy the Temple? The Temple authorities were all about keeping things the "same," but Jesus was about making the world different. To those wanting to uphold the status quo, "different" was threatening. It was then that their decision became firm. They needed somehow to get rid of Jesus. To have him executed would get rid of "the problem" for good.

As many already were making the journey to Jerusalem early to prepare for the Passover, which would begin soon, Jesus hid in the town of Ephraim: "Therefore Jesus no longer moved about publicly among the people of Judea. Instead, he withdrew to a region near the wilderness, to a village called Ephraim, where he stayed with his disciples. … The chief priests and the Pharisees had given orders that anyone who found out where Jesus was should report it so that they might arrest him" (John 11:54, 57). The people of Ephraim protected Jesus. He would stay hidden away all of this week—up until he would make his way back to Lazarus' home in Bethany near Judea for the last time, the time of his final anointing. From there, he would make his way to Jerusalem, and his time of "reckoning" would commence.

Story

Jesus Is the Bread of Life

[After Jesus fed the 5,000 men plus women and children, and once] the crowd realized that neither Jesus nor his disciples were there, they got into the boats and went to Capernaum in search of Jesus.

When they found him on the other side of the lake, they asked him, "Rabbi, when did you get here?"

Jesus answered, "Very truly I tell you, you are looking for me, not because you saw the signs I performed but because you ate the loaves and had your fill. Do not work for food that spoils, but for food that endures to eternal life, which the Son of Man will give you. For on him God the Father has placed his seal of approval."

Then they asked him, "What must we do to do the works God requires?"

Jesus answered, "The work of God is this: to believe in the one He has sent."

So they asked him, "What sign then will you give that we may see it and believe you? What will you do? Our ancestors ate the manna in the wilderness; as it is written: 'He gave them bread from heaven to eat.'"

Jesus said to them, "Very truly I tell you, it is not Moses who has given you the bread from heaven, but it is my Father who gives you the true bread from heaven. For the bread of God is the bread that comes down from heaven and gives life to the world."

"Sir," they said, "always give us this bread."

Then Jesus declared, "I am the bread of life. Whoever comes to me will never go hungry, and whoever believes in me will never be thirsty. But as I told you, you have seen me and still you do not believe. All those the Father gives me will come to me, and whoever comes to me I will never drive away. For I have come down from heaven not to do my will but to do the will of Him who sent me. And this is the will of Him who sent me, that I shall lose none of all those He has given me, but raise them up at the last day. For my Father's will is that everyone who looks to the Son and believes in him shall have eternal life, and I will raise them up at the last day."

At this the Jews there began to grumble about him because he said, "I am the bread that came down from heaven." They said, "Is this not

Jesus, the son of Joseph, whose father and mother we know? How can he now say, 'I came down from heaven?'"

"Stop grumbling among yourselves," Jesus answered. "No one can come to me unless the Father who sent me draws them, and I will raise them up at the last day. It is written in the Prophets: 'They will all be taught by God.' Everyone who has heard the Father and learned from him comes to me. No one has seen the Father except the one who is from God; only he has seen the Father. Very truly I tell you, the one who believes has eternal life. I am the bread of life. Your ancestors ate the manna in the wilderness, yet they died. But here is the bread that comes down from heaven, which anyone may eat and not die. I am the living bread that came down from heaven. Whoever eats this bread will live forever. This bread is my flesh, which I will give for the life of the world."

Then the Jews began to argue sharply among themselves, "How can this man give us his flesh to eat?"

Jesus said to them, "Very truly I tell you, unless you eat the flesh of the Son of Man and drink his blood, you have no life in you. Whoever eats my flesh and drinks my blood has eternal life, and I will raise them up at the last day. For my flesh is real food and my blood is real drink. Whoever eats my flesh and drinks my blood remains in me, and I in them. Just as the living Father sent me and I live because of the Father, so the one who feeds on me will live because of me. This is the bread that came down from heaven. Your ancestors ate manna and died, but whoever feeds on this bread will live forever." He said this while teaching in the synagogue in Capernaum.

On hearing it, many of his disciples said, "This is a hard teaching. Who can accept it?"

Aware that his disciples were grumbling about this, Jesus said to them, "Does this offend you? Then what if you see the Son of Man ascend to where he was before! The Spirit gives life; the flesh counts for nothing. The words I have spoken to you—they are full of the Spirit and life. Yet there are some of you who do not believe." For Jesus had known from the beginning which of them did not believe and who would betray him. He went on to say, "This is why I told you that no one can come to me unless the Father has enabled them."

From this time many of his disciples turned back and no longer followed him.

"You do not want to leave too, do you?" Jesus asked the Twelve.

Simon Peter answered him, "Lord, to whom shall we go? You have the words of eternal life. We have come to believe and to know that you are the Holy One of God."

Then Jesus replied, "Have I not chosen you, the Twelve? Yet one of you is a devil!" (He meant Judas, the son of Simon Iscariot, who, though one of the Twelve, was later to betray him) (John 6:24–71).

Imagine

Often, when it came to understanding Jesus, the disciples were a few peas short of a casserole. They were used to thinking literally, and Jesus was used to talking in metaphors that required a bit more depth.

One day, after the Pharisees and Sadducees had spent some time in a verbal duel with Jesus, trying to trip him up, Jesus wanted to explain to his disciples something about the nature of these pompous scholars.

Now the disciples had just come across the Sea of Galilee to meet Jesus, and when they arrived there, they realized that they had forgotten to bring any bread with them. And so, they were feeling a bit worried about what Jesus might say to them. When Jesus began to talk to them about the Temple establishment, warning them to beware of the "leaven" of the Pharisees and Sadducees, the disciples weren't sure what he meant. They mumbled to each other, "Jesus must mean we shouldn't buy bread from a baker who associates with the Pharisees or Sadducees. He must have said that because we showed up without any bread!" You see, the idea that being a devout

Jew meant you were careful about whom you associated with was so ingrained in the disciples that they immediately jumped to this default.

But Jesus caught on to what they were muttering about, and he addressed them right away: "Do you really think that I care which baker you patronize? Don't you still understand the way I teach? Even after spending so much time as my disciples? So, you showed up without any bread. So what? Don't you remember that we fed five thousand people before with only five rounds of flatbread? Don't you remember the excess we had afterward? When I am talking about 'leaven,' I'm not talking about what we will eat for dinner! I will say it again: Avoid the leaven of the Pharisees and Sadducees."

Finally, the disciples got it! Jesus didn't mean the bread you literally eat, but the "food that feeds your soul." He was speaking in metaphor. He was warning them against following the ways of the Pharisees and Sadducees.

Jesus uses "leaven" in two ways. Earlier, he had offered them a parable about the kingdom of heaven and described it as "leaven." Now he was warning them about the "leaven" of the Pharisees and Sadducees.

Table Talk

>🜚 What do you think Jesus means by "leaven"?

>🜚 What kind of "leaven" does Jesus want us to cultivate? How do you think you can have "leaven" in your own life?

>🜚 What does it mean to avoid the "leaven" of our current culture? Who are the "Pharisees" of today? Or the Sadducees?

>🜚 Jesus also talked about the importance of having salt within. What do you think he meant?

➢ Jesus said he is the Bread of Life. What does that mean to you?

Roundtable Relational Activity

Think creatively. With your sisters and brothers around the table with Jesus, make a "salt covenant" together. What will it mean to make this discipleship covenant with Jesus and with your brothers and sisters in Christ? How will you be accountable to each other in love? Say a prayer to seal your vow.

Lenten Challenge

This week, be the kind of salty leaven that Jesus hopes you can be. Do something nice for a stranger. Buy someone coffee. Pay the bill of the person behind you or ahead of you in line. Leave an extra tip. Give someone else the best seat ahead of you. Stop to help someone struggling. Strike up a conversation with someone sitting beside you on the bus.

Record your experiments in your Lenten Journal. What happened?

Meal

Enjoy your meal of stew and bread. As you sip your wine or juice at the table with Jesus, and you express your desire to follow him, he asks you, "Can you drink from my cup?"

Jesus explains that it will be a hard road for his disciples to follow if they see the world in terms of the way everyone else does. He needs you to see differently. Can you handle looking different to the world? Can you keep your eyes straight when others look at you sideways?

Jesus' cup is the cup of transformation. But it is also a cup of sacrifice. Can you be a "blood" brother or sister? Jesus asks, "Will you be there for me when my blood flows?"

If you can, put down your glass, take Jesus' hand, and pledge yourself to him for life.

Closing Prayer

Lord, make me a disciple of the "cup"—a follower in your path and a lover of your people. Help me to immerse myself deeply in relationship with you, so that I understand not just with my mind, but through my faith. I know that my life can be made perfect only in you. Give me rest from my urges to make things "good" for myself. Give me the faith to know that when I am with you, I am already everything I need to be, that "Christ in me" is more than good. It is exquisitely beautiful. Amen.

Jew or Greek

Menu: *Greek Pasticcio, Green Beans with Tomatoes, Red Wine or Grape Juice*

Recipe: *Cook onion until it becomes transparent. Add ground meat seasoned with pepper, salt, and fragrant cinnamon. Add some tomato puree and butter and cook. Stir in a half cup of seasoned breadcrumbs and set aside. Prepare a white sauce by heating butter. Add flour, salt, and pepper. Then add milk with egg yolk. Simmer and set aside. Prepare cooked macaroni. When done, mix into it melted butter and grated cheese. In a large pan, sprinkle the bottom with seasoned crumbs, then pour in macaroni and spread. Over it, spread the ground meat, and then more macaroni. Pour white sauce over it and top with remaining cheese. Bake 1 hour. Cook green beans with seasoned tomato sauce and marjoram.*

Shopping List: *onion, ground meat, cinnamon, tomato puree, butter, seasoned breadcrumbs, flour, 1 egg, milk, macaroni, grated cheese, green beans, cans of seasoned tomato sauce, marjoram.*

Prayer

Lord, help me to see people the way you do. Give me the courage to walk with you through unknown places and to embrace unknown people. Give me the faith of Bartimaeus, the zeal of Zacchaeus, and a passion to serve in the world with you. Amen.

Backdrop/Geographical Portrait

After spending time hidden away in quiet with his disciples in the outskirts of Ephraim, today Jesus is on the move. He prepares to make his way back to Judea. He knows this involves significant risk, but he also knows it's what he needs to do. Jericho is about an hour or so (five miles) away. It's Jesus' first stop. Here he will encounter Zacchaeus and Bartimaeus.

Jesus will dine with Zacchaeus, the tax collector, in the "tax capital" of the ancient region, and Zacchaeus will experience a conversion (something Jesus could not do with the Jewish money changers in the Jerusalem Temple).

Later Jesus will spend some public time healing blindness back on the road. It is here that he meets Bartimaeus and brings at least one more disciple to "sight," a faith that he would not encounter with the Jewish Pharisees, or with many of his own disciples. Even the thief on the cross is converted when Jesus' own disciple Judas (his treasurer and a thief in his own right) could not be moved. In fact, Jesus' entire time in Jericho, the "Garden City," is about "seeing"—coming to faith and seeking and finding relationship with God: "For the Son of Man came to seek and to save the lost" (Luke 19:10).

This will be the last chance for many to "see" the truth of the gospel before Jesus wraps up his public ministry and moves from Son to Savior.

Jericho, across the Jordan River, was known as the "City of Palms." But the name "Jericho" literally means "the perfumed." Josephus describes the town in the fertile area of the Jordan as the "little Paradise." Gardens of palms, roses, balsam ... the entire city gave off a sweet scent of perfume. It was the "Eden of Palestine." Here, in this gentile city of Herod, Jesus encountered more faith than he would in Jerusalem, the city of his tears.

Story

Jesus Heals Bartimaeus

Jesus and his disciples went to Jericho. And as they were leaving, they were followed by a large crowd. A blind beggar by the name of Bartimaeus son of Timaeus was sitting beside the road. When he heard that it was Jesus from Nazareth, he shouted, "Jesus, Son of David, have pity on me!"

Many people told the man to stop, but he shouted even louder, "Son of David, have pity on me!"

Jesus stopped and said, "Call him over!"

They called out to the blind man and said, "Don't be afraid! Come on! He is calling for you."

The man threw off his coat as he jumped up and ran to Jesus.

Jesus asked, "What do you want me to do for you?"

The blind man answered, "Master, I want to see!"

Jesus told him, "You may go. Your eyes are healed because of your faith."

Right away the man could see, and he went down the road with Jesus. (Mark 10:46-52 CEV).

Imagine

It will be another four to five hours from Jericho to Bethany, and a bit less than an hour from Bethany to Jerusalem (two miles). Jesus will leave on his way to Bethany in the morning. After his "perfumed anointing," he will ride the "palm strewn" way into Jerusalem for the Feast of Unleavened Bread.

As Jesus is preparing to wrap up his earthly and natural mission, he is also preparing the way for his supernatural miracle—a cataclysm of such immense proportions that it would rock the world and start in motion a "kingdom" that would have no bounds and could not be tamed.

From now on, Jesus is on the "move" and "on the lam." Will you join him as he walks this road? The journey has only just begun.

We all know the story of Joshua and the falling of Jericho's walls, the separating barrier between the Israelites' past and their new future. Their entry through Jericho would begin Israel's time in the Lord's promised land.

Jesus encounters lots of "walls" and "barriers" in his ministry and mission too. The power of faith is highlighted in Jesus' final visit to the city of Jericho as he reenters Judea. His visit is permeated by collapsing walls of doubt and separation. More walls came down in that one day than would in Jesus' week leading to his death.

Concealment can keep us from allowing Jesus to heal us the way we need to be healed in order to be made whole in God. All of us have walls we build around our hearts, around our spirits, within our minds, and within our lives. Some walls may come from negative past experiences. Some may come from difficulties in our interactions with others. Some may come from resistance to intimacy. All are rooted in some way in fear: fear of intimacy, fear of letting go of control, fear of authenticity, fear of surrender. Fear inhibits your ability to trust.

But Jesus the beautiful healer comes to us unconcealed. If we approach Jesus wanting to be healed, we can give Jesus license to break through, break down, and break away our walls. We cannot "see" when we've got "logs" in our eyes. If you allow Jesus to heal you, his journey will touch you, challenge you, and empower you in ways you have never experienced before.

Table Talk

> ↪ What walls do you keep between Jesus and you? What walls do you think keep you from telling others about Jesus' gift of Life? What barriers do you sense in your life? In your relationships?

➣ Today, can you put aside your fears and let Jesus remove the obstacles that are keeping you from surrendering in trust to the Lord?

➣ Blindness is another metaphor for "not seeing," for remaining concealed. In what ways do you feel you are blind to the way others see you or feel about you? In what ways would your relationships change if you opened your eyes to see others as people as fearful as you?

➣ What does Jesus' ministry of healing say about his mission to the gentiles?

➣ How do you think Jesus defines being part of the "true" Israel of God?

Roundtable Relational Activity

Today, allow yourself to be blindfolded. Allow someone else to feed you. Then do the same for someone else. Feel the trust that you must make in giving up the control of your own feeding. How do you feel? Why do you think you feel the way you do?

Now imagine it is Jesus feeding you. Allow yourself to lose your fear and embrace your relationship with the risen Christ. Then, rise up and follow him to Bethany.

Lenten Challenge

Make a dish or casserole of food and deliver it to someone who could use a break this week. Often, we do this only when someone is mourning in some way, grieving a death, or sick. But we are all in need of "acts of kindness" for no particular reason. A gift of food can nurture someone's soul, elicit a smile, and foster a relationship.

Describe in your Lenten Journal how that person reacted to your gift. How has it changed or nurtured the relationship between you?

Meal

Foods are aromatic, some more than others. Before you dine, take a moment to close your eyes and breathe in the aromas of the food before you. What scents can you identify?

Each of us may respond differently to the aromas around us. When we are called by God, and each of us are, each in a different and unique way, we embody that call as a sweetness of our spirit. As we incarnate the Spirit of Christ within us, the food of the gospel becomes a fragrant and fulfilling truth within us. Our words, our actions, our love, and our faith waft forth into the world so that others might respond to Jesus through us.

Say a prayer that as you partake of this food, you invite Jesus to reside within your heart.

Closing Prayer

Lord, take away the inhibitions that keep me solitary and fearful. With your mighty voice, break away my walls. Let the scales from my eyes fall away. Lift me into the Truth of your presence. Make me whole. Amen.

You Will Know Them by Their Fruits / The Procession of the Lambs

Menu: *Mediterranean Couscous with Figs and Olives, Lamb (or Beef) Kababs, Red Wine or Grape Juice*

Recipe: *Make a fragrant couscous with figs and olives, and the Mediterranean spices and herbs of your choice, including cilantro. Prepare balls of either ground lamb or beef mixed with onion and cinnamon. (You can also prepare this with cubes of meat.) Mix in Mediterranean spice and seasoned breadcrumbs. If using cubes, rub with Mediterranean spices or garam masala. Bake or barbecue over a fire. Serve with olives.*

Shopping List: *couscous, figs, olives, Mediterranean spices, cilantro, ground beef or lamb, onion, cinnamon, seasoned breadcrumbs, optional garam masala.*

Prayer

Lord Creator God, you created a living world that can feed and nourish us in body, mind, and spirit. Thank you for your gifts—the trees of the field, the fruits of the vine, meat, fish. May my life be as that food: consecrated to you. Lord, let it all be good. Amen.

Backdrop/Geographical Portrait

Olives are a staple of Mediterranean life. But the olive tree can be a finicky tree to grow. A lot depends on its environment and its tending. Even in its native soil, the tree is sensitive to conditions, yields little, and takes a long time to mature. When it does, the fruit must be hand-harvested. The odd thing about the olive tree is that it does not survive well in rich soil, but it thrives in rocky, dry, nutrient-deficient landscapes. Fruit-bearing age depends on its cultivation, but usually it takes at least four years to see fruit emerge. Some take many years to bear fruit. The more mature the plant, the more fruit it bears. But once it flourishes, it stands forever. Even if cut back or cut down—yes, even if burnt down—the olive tree, its roots once established, will always grow back!

"I am like an olive tree flourishing in the house of God," says the psalmist (Psalm 52:8). What a statement of praise by someone with roots deeply and long invested in the Lord!

Today, olive trees in the Garden of Gethsemane in the region of Jerusalem still grow and flourish. Some are nine hundred years old and date from the twelfth century, although their roots prove much older still and date to about 1092. DNA analysis points to evidence that the eight trees currently living date back to the roots of an earlier, even older single tree (approximately three thousand years old), one that may have shielded Jesus as he prayed and sweated blood in that garden before his ordeal.

The Mount of Olives was Jesus' favorite place to pray outside of the city of Jerusalem, where he spent his last evenings the week of his death. Gethsemane (*geth* and *shemen*) means "oil press." This area is thought to be the origin of the tree of life. In Jesus' parable regarding the vineyard of olives, the trees must be nourished, pruned, and diligently cared for in order for them to bear good fruit.

The fig tree also has a rich scriptural history. Near the end of Jesus' ministry, he curses a fig tree. But why? The fig tree has long been a symbol of Israel. But Jesus' contemporaries for the most part did not understand what it meant to be God's "Israel." They thought it meant that they had the "right" biological lineage, that they followed the Law in the correct ways, or that they belonged to the "right" families. Jesus tells us that the fig tree is a symbol of a loving heart in covenant with God. The fig tree is the hope for Jerusalem, a time when everyone will sit under his or her own fig tree. The kingdom of God comes from a heart entwined with the True Vine and rooted in the Holy Spirit of God's love, forgiveness, kindness, and mercy.

Story

Jesus Prepares for the Procession of the Lambs

As they approached Jerusalem and came to Bethphage and Bethany at the Mount of Olives, Jesus sent two of his disciples, saying to them, "Go to the village ahead of you, and just as you enter it, you will find a colt tied there, which no one has ever ridden. Untie it and bring it here. If anyone asks you, 'Why are you doing this?' say, 'The Lord needs it and will send it back here shortly.'"

They went and found a colt outside in the street, tied at a doorway. As they untied it, some people standing there asked, "What are you do-ing, untying that colt?" They answered as Jesus had told them to, and the people let them go. When they brought the colt to Jesus and threw their cloaks over it, he sat on it. Many people spread their cloaks on the road, while others spread branches they had cut in the fields. Those who went ahead and those who followed shouted,

"Hosanna!"

"Blessed is he who comes in the name of the Lord!"

"Blessed is the coming kingdom of our father David!"

"Hosanna in the highest heaven!"

Jesus entered Jerusalem and went into the temple courts. He looked around at everything, but since it was already late, he went out to Bethany with the Twelve.

The next day as they were leaving Bethany, Jesus was hungry. Seeing in the distance a fig tree in leaf, he went to find out if it had any fruit. When he reached it, he found nothing but leaves, because it was not the season for figs. Then he said to the tree, "May no one ever eat fruit from you again." And his disciples heard him say it.

On reaching Jerusalem, Jesus entered the temple courts and began driving out those who were buying and selling there. He overturned the tables of the money changers and the benches of those selling doves and would not allow anyone to carry merchandise through the temple courts. And as he taught them, he said, "Is it not written: 'My house will be called a house of prayer for all nations'? But you have made it 'a den of robbers.'"

The chief priests and the teachers of the law heard this and began looking for a way to kill him, for they feared him, because the whole crowd was amazed at his teaching.

When evening came, Jesus and his disciples went out of the city.

In the morning, as they went along, they saw the fig tree withered from the roots. Peter remembered and said to Jesus, "Rabbi, look! The fig tree you cursed has withered!"

"Have faith in God," Jesus answered. "Truly I tell you, if anyone says to this mountain, 'Go, throw yourself into the sea,' and does not doubt in their heart but believes that what they say will happen, it will be done for them. Therefore I tell you, whatever you ask for in prayer, believe that you have received it, and it will be yours. And when you stand praying, if you hold anything against anyone, forgive them, so that your Father in heaven may forgive you your sins."

They arrived again in Jerusalem, and while Jesus was walking in the temple courts, the chief priests, the teachers of the law and the elders came to him. "By what authority are you doing these things?" they asked. "And who gave you authority to do this?"

Jesus replied, "I will ask you one question. Answer me, and I will tell you by what authority I am doing these things. John's baptism—was it from heaven, or of human origin? Tell me!"

They discussed it among themselves and said, "If we say, 'From heaven,' he will ask, 'Then why didn't you believe him?' But if we say, 'Of human origin' ..." (They feared the people, for everyone held that John really was a prophet.)

So they answered Jesus, "We don't know."

Jesus said, "Neither will I tell you by what authority I am doing these things" (Mark 11).

Imagine

"Turn away from me; let me weep bitterly. Do not try to console me over the destruction of my people" (Isaiah 22:4).

"As he approached Jerusalem and saw the city, [Jesus] wept over it" (Luke 19:41).

There is no better place in the Scriptures to see Jesus' humanity than in his fervent desire to save his people. All people. But even Jesus knew he couldn't save them all. Still, it never stopped him from fulfilling his mission in order to save the ones he could.

As a disciple of the Lord, you too may sometimes feel you do very little within the world. But if you have touched even one life with the healing touch of the Savior, if you have allowed even one person to find peace and joy in the gospel, if you have given the gift of Christ's overwhelming grace to even one, you have already done so very much.

At the table today, as you dine with your Lord and Savior, know that he is crying along with you for all those in the world whose lives remain broken, all those who find it difficult to see, all those who are not yet safe within his loving arms.

Pray with him. Weep with him. Then go out and save the ones you can.

Table Talk

- ✐ Who do you have great compassion for in your community? In the world?

- ✐ Can you have compassion for those who make you angry? For those who have harmed you?

- ✐ We know that people need companionship, connection, and a sense of belonging to feel okay about themselves and others. How can you foster connections and relationships in your community?

- ✐ What are ways to ease someone's anger and to help them see Jesus in you?

- ✐ "By their fruit you will recognize them," Jesus reminds us (Matthew 7:20). What do you think the fruits of the Spirit look like in people today? Give an example of when you recognized that kind of fruit, that deep rootedness in Jesus, within someone in your life.

- ✐ Can you feel Jesus urging and nourishing you, as he does for all humanity? Can you feel the presence of the gardener seeking to secure your roots and guide your branches?

Roundtable Relational Activity

Go around the table and tell the group something about the person next to you—the qualities you admire, the value you see in that person's faith, and what that person means to you.

How did it feel to do that? What kind of bond did you feel growing between you and the person next to you? How has it changed your relationship?

Lenten Challenge

Create a fruit basket with your favorite fruits. Take it to someone you don't know. You might drop it at the post office and thank the postal worker for his or her great work on behalf of your community. Or you might take it to someone in the hospital. Perhaps you can greet a neighbor just because you never had the chance to get to know him or her before.

Describe in your journal what "fruits of the Spirit" you utilized in giving this gift. Describe the reaction of the person or people to whom you gave your gift.

Meal

As you share in your meal together today, talk among each other and with Jesus about what it means to sow the seeds of the gospel in the lives of others. How can we better make our lives a journey of seed sowing, planting, and investing in the life of Jesus?

Closing Prayer

Lord, let my heart be rooted in you. Help my faith spread like the branches of the olive tree. Bless my life to bear fruit in your name. Amen.

[Optional: You might want to use Holy Week for fasting or simple finger foods, such as olives, hummus, unleavened bread, and grape juice, or use this week to do a reenactment of the Jewish Seder, followed by Holy Communion. Make this a prayer gathering in which you put everyday ritual aside and take on the mood of mourning, fasting, and conversation about Jesus' last walk.]

The Good Shepherd

> **Menu:** *Shepherd's Pie, Mediterranean Salad, Red Wine or Grape Juice*
>
> **Recipe:** *Mash cooked potatoes and mix with parsley, onions, and matzo crumbs. Add pepper mixed with lamb meat. Add tomato sauce, butter, rosemary, thyme, cinnamon, oregano, and matzo crumbs. Fold in cooked carrots and peas. Bake at 400 for one hour. Create a salad with greens, olives, tomatoes, and goat cheese. Drizzle with olive oil, pepper, cilantro, and a small amount of red wine vinegar. Serve with wine or juice.*
>
> **Shopping List:** *potatoes, parsley, onions, matzo, lamb meat (beef can be substituted), rosemary, thyme, cinnamon, oregano, carrots and peas (frozen is fine), greens, olives, tomatoes, goat cheese, cilantro, olive oil, red wine vinegar.*

Prayer

Lord, prepare me to be a servant of your kingdom. Give me the strength to serve well, the passion to serve with ardor, and the love to serve with grace. Amen.

Backdrop/Geographical Portrait

Bethlehem means in Hebrew "house of bread," and in Aramaic/Arabic "house of meat." On the hillsides of Bethlehem, where David was once a shepherd, graze the lambs that will be used in the Passover sacrifices. They are carefully reared, cared for, and coddled so that they will be perfect and without blemish, as that is the requirement for the sacrificial presentation in the Temple for each family.

Several days before Passover, each family has to choose a lamb, bring it into their home, and treat it as their family, for a sacrifice is not a sacrifice unless it is something you love. The lamb they will sacrifice will atone for the sins of the entire family for the upcoming year.

Jesus calls himself the Good Shepherd, but also the Lamb of God. He cares for God's flocks, but he is also the sacrificial Lamb, led to slaughter. His sacrifice will atone for the sins of the entire world for all eternity. All who follow his voice as "gatekeeper" will enter into the Kingdom of Heaven. Jesus is the Lamb victorious and the Shepherd of all of Israel—the "true" Israel, all those whose "hearts" belong to God. For Jesus, faith defines your identity. Trusting in him makes you Israel's child.

Story

"I am the Good Shepherd."

"Very truly I tell you Pharisees, anyone who does not enter the sheep pen by the gate, but climbs in by some other way, is a thief and a robber. The one who enters by the gate is the shepherd of the sheep. The gatekeeper opens the gate for him, and the sheep listen to his voice. He calls his own sheep by name and leads them out. When he has brought out all his own, he goes on ahead of them, and his sheep follow him because they know his voice. But they will never follow a stranger; in fact, they will run away from him because they do not recognize a stranger's voice." Jesus used this figure of speech, but the Pharisees did not understand what he was telling them.

Therefore, Jesus said again, "Very truly I tell you, I am the gate for the sheep. All who have come before me are thieves and robbers, but the sheep have not listened to them. I am the gate; whoever enters through me will be saved. They will come in and go out, and find pasture. The thief comes only to steal and kill and destroy; I have come that they may have life, and have it to the full.

"I am the good shepherd. The good shepherd lays down his life for the sheep. The hired hand is not the shepherd and does not own the sheep. So when he sees the wolf coming, he abandons the sheep and runs away. Then the wolf attacks the flock and scatters it. The man runs away because he is a hired hand and cares nothing for the sheep.

"I am the good shepherd; I know my sheep and my sheep know me— just as the Father knows me and I know the Father—and I lay down my life for the sheep. I have other sheep that are not of this sheep pen. I must bring them also. They too will listen to my voice, and there shall be one flock and one shepherd. The reason my Father loves me is that I lay down my life—only to take it up again. No one takes it from me, but I lay it down of my own accord. I have authority to lay it down and authority to take it up again. This command I received from my Father."

The Jews who heard these words were again divided. Many of them said, "He is demon-possessed and raving mad. Why listen to him?"

But others said, "These are not the sayings of a man possessed by a demon. Can a demon open the eyes of the blind?"

Then came the Festival of Dedication at Jerusalem. It was winter, and Jesus was in the temple courts walking in Solomon's Colonnade. The Jews who were there gathered around him, saying, "How long will you keep us in suspense? If you are the Messiah, tell us plainly."

Jesus answered, "I did tell you, but you do not believe. The works I do in my Father's name testify about me, but you do not believe because you are not my sheep. My sheep listen to my voice; I know them, and they follow me. I give them eternal life, and they shall never perish; no one will snatch them out of my hand. My Father, who has given them to me, is greater than all; no one can snatch them out of my Father's hand. I and the Father are one."

Again his Jewish opponents picked up stones to stone him, but Jesus said to them, "I have shown you many good works from the Father. For which of these do you stone me?"

"We are not stoning you for any good work," they replied, "but for blasphemy, because you, a mere man, claim to be God."

Jesus answered them, "Is it not written in your Law, 'I have said you are "gods"'? If he called them 'gods,' to whom the word of God came—and Scripture cannot be set aside—what about the one whom the Father set apart as his very own and sent into the world? Why then do you accuse me of blasphemy because I said, 'I am God's Son'? Do not believe me unless I do the works of my Father. But if I do them, even though you do not believe me, believe the works, that you may know and understand that the Father is in me, and I in the Father." Again they tried to seize him, but he escaped their grasp (John 10:1–39).

Imagine

Today you will help Martha prepare a shepherd's pie for the meal of the day before Jesus starts on his way to Jerusalem. Jesus and his disciples will be hungry after their days on the road, and you want to be prepared. You can hear the sounds of the crowd already gathered in Jerusalem at the Northern Gate. They've gathered bunches of palm fronds, along with branches of other native trees.

After the procession, all of the families will take their chosen animal into their homes to await the day of sacrifice, when the Paschal lamb will be slain and the meat prepared for the High Feast.

Around the table are many of Jesus' supporters and benefactors, even some Pharisees, who believe Jesus to be the long-awaited Messiah. But what the messiah is to be and do is a matter of disagreement and dispute among them, even among Jesus' closest disciples.

The events of this supper will mean a final turning point for many of Jesus' followers. A straw will be broken. Does Jesus really think it kosher to be lavished with a $20,000 jar of expensive anointing oil, when a year's worth of money could have gone to the poor? Or to fund the future ministry of the group? How can he allow this? Why doesn't he chastise Mary?

Many feel they have misunderstood him. He is beginning to say things that are harder and harder to understand. Some feel betrayed, others confused, and others simply afraid, for they see he is preparing for his death, that he means to allow it to happen.

Judas will be determined to halt Jesus' reckless abandon of Jewish values and bring this notorious, extravagant, and outlandish ministry to an end, especially when it threatens the making of money under the table, as Judas has a habit of helping himself to portions of the mission's purse.

Judas may think he is preventing Jesus from going off the deep end. Little does he know that once he sells Jesus into the hands of the authorities, he will also sell his own soul.

No one will understand truly who Jesus is until after the resurrection. For now, Jesus tells them he is the true shepherd, the Good Shepherd—God's shepherd of the true Israel (all those who will follow him through the gates and into God's waiting arms).

Table Talk

- How has money gotten in the way of your ministry in the past? Of your church's ministry and mission?

- What does it mean for Jesus to be a Shepherd King or Shepherd Messiah?

- What are the qualities of a "shepherd"? Talk about this around your table today.

Roundtable Relational Activity

Who are you at this final table with Jesus? What do you think about his strange talk and behavior? Talk with each other about what Jesus tells you is to come. Will you follow him to the cross? What do you think he is asking of you still today?

Lenten Challenge

As you move into Holy Week, as you emerge from it and into Jesus' resurrection moment, allow yourself to feel his journey. Walk it with him. We cannot feel the extravagant joy of Jesus' resurrection life until we have experienced the utter grief of his cross and tomb.

Journal throughout the week. Think about what Jesus was experiencing in that week, his frustration, his sadness, his failures, and his final victory. In what ways have you felt failure and frustration in your ministry or mission? In what way does Jesus' resurrection provide you hope for your life and the life of your church?

Meal

You are entering into a time of waiting. As you share Martha's Shepherd's Pie together, think of that barren fig tree. For now, the tree lays barren and withered, but it will bloom again. As from the beginning of time, God will begin again with His people. Share the words of Psalm 118:22: "The stone the builders rejected has become the cornerstone." What does this mean for you?

Closing Prayer

Lord, give me strength to endure what is to come in my life and in my faith. Challenge me to walk with you, to follow you into difficult places, and to live out the gospel in the world, even in a world that does not understand your gift. Amen.

Around the Table
with Jesus

24 Days to Resurrection: A Lenten Devotional

These devotionals can also be used for an entire forty-eight days of Lent.

Will you join me for a twenty-four-day "fast" before Easter? Cleanse your body and your soul with daily times of "breaking bread" with Jesus. I invite you to walk with me, with each other, and with Christ through these days before the celebration of the resurrection, making each meal a prayer for God's grace in body and spirit. As Christ walked his final days to the cross, his faith, resolve, and trust in the Father grew ever stronger, so as to sustain him in his final mission of victory. Let your body and heart too be strengthened and sustained in Christ.

Thank you for joining me. Each day, you will find meal suggestions for breakfast, lunch, and supper. The idea is to drink only water in between and to consume only the suggested meal. For each meal, I invite you to read the short meditation or prayer for that meal as you spend "time" and "space" in relationship with Jesus. The meals will be lean, simple, and high in fiber (Mediterranean). As these meals are designed as a healthy and relational "means of grace," I hope you will find yourself refreshed and renewed in body and mind, even as your spirit is refreshed and renewed by your time with Christ. I hope you'll join me as I join with Jesus on this walk to strength and life.

24 Days to Resurrection

BREAKFAST WITH JESUS

Break your fast with a "feast"—a bowl of fresh fruit, some yo-gurt, and coffee or tea.

If you are used to a larger breakfast and must move gradually into your "fast," add some cereal into your yogurt or add a slice of whole grain toast or a bagel with cream cheese. In place of coffee or tea, add an eight-ounce glass of milk or Ovaltine.

On this first day, imagine Jesus with you at your table. As you enjoy your fruit, fresh from the tree, and you revel in its flavor and juice, you and Jesus lift your glasses and toast to your relationship, to the walk you will take with him. Your "fast" is a celebration, your meal not the dregs of water and bread, but the succulent and lavish fruits of the Spirit.

While you are laughing and talking with Jesus, someone taps him on the shoulder for a moment and whispers in a low voice so you can hear: "What's wrong with you? Why are you and your dis-ciples celebrating like this, when others are fasting rather than feast-ing, saying prayers rather than drinking and laughing together over coffee?" Jesus says to them, "Imagine there's a wedding going on. Would you ignore the bridegroom's festivities and fast instead? Those who've never tasted something new in a new way won't know what they're missing. They'll always say, 'The old way is good enough for me!' But I am offering you a new way."

Make today the start of a "new way" of feasting with Jesus. Celebrate this walk with him.

Prayer

Lord, I begin this day fresh with you. I pray that as I share this walk with you, each step will bring me closer to you in body, mind, and spirit. Amen.

LUNCHTIME WITH JESUS

Take a lunchtime break and take a short walk with Jesus. Look around you. What signs of livingness do you see, even in this time of fall or winter?

Hear Jesus' voice: "Just look at those beautiful wild lilies growing over there. Look at the grass, how it strives merely to live. It's so fresh and beautiful. You don't need to pursue an extravagant lifestyle or planned-out food and drink. Your mind doesn't need to be filled with angst or worry over what to eat and not to eat. Just pursue a relationship with me first and foremost, and everything else in life will come together for you."

This lunchtime, take a short walk. On the way, take time to pay attention to the sights and sounds around you that you miss when you are focused on work and all of the distractions of your everyday life. Take time to feel how alive you are. Take time to feel Christ's hand in yours walking along the way. Then come back and heat some simple soup for lunch. No complicated preparation necessary; no need for assembling lots of things. Perhaps you'll choose a bowl of tomato or broccoli soup sprinkled with a bit of basil or thyme. A cauliflower soup laced with a hint of saffron might remind you of the little bits of grace that change the flavor of your life. Even a simple chicken soup can be edged with a bit of chili or red pepper. Allow this meal with its edgy preparation to infuse some creative passion into your Lenten journey. If you dare, include a glass of V-8 spiked with a splash of hot sauce. Add an apple or banana that you find lurking in your basket of goodness, and a lot of Living Water.

Prayer

Lord, thank you for this daily "bread"—the companionship of your presence, the strength of your sustenance, the simplicity of faith. Amen.

SUPPER WITH JESUS

Tonight, on this first day of your Lenten journey, I recommend to you a dish of roasted vegetables: perhaps some mushrooms, tomatoes, broccoli, zucchini, carrots, or onions. Perhaps even some turnips, asparagus, eggplant, or potatoes. Sprinkle them with a little salt and pepper and toss them with olive oil. Roast them for 20 minutes and season them with some rosemary. Along with them, prepare some Mediterranean fish. Bake it with a little onion, diced tomatoes, and thyme. Add another toss of olive oil and bake for 25 minutes. Pour a bit of apple cider into sparkling water and add a bit of mint and basil.

Imagine Jesus there with you as you prepare for supper. He reminds you to remember what is real and important for your life, not what your eyes find desirable or what you imagine you need as a substitute or "sugar-fix." He invites you to remember the people who mean the most, the relationships that feed your soul. If you pay attention closely, you will hear Jesus in your kitchen, preparing you the meal of your childhood that you most love, the food that nourishes you most, the dish that tastes most like home. You remember that you love it, not just because it tastes good, but because sometime in your life, it was prepared and served by someone you love. Your mind remembers the familiar tastes and smells, the ones that came wafting down the hall or up the stairs calling you to the table with family and friends. As you are eating your meal tonight, remember those who have been important, inviting, and nourishing in your life. Now come to Jesus. He is waiting.

Jesus says, "Seek out the kind of food that will be of lasting value in your life, the spiritual food that comes from me, the one on whom God the Father has placed his own seal of approval." Supper is "around the table time." Whether alone or with family or friends, don't forget to invite Jesus to your table. Make conversation with Jesus your "table talk" tonight. While you are nourishing your body, nourish your spirit with prayer. Relish each bite. Breathe in the scent. Tasting food can be a kind of tangible prayer. Savor each bite slowly. Experience the various notes within your food. Be nourished body, mind, and spirit.

Prayer

Lord Jesus, you are my home. My soul finds nourishment in you, and with you I am filled and fulfilled. Amen.

24 Days to Resurrection

BREAKFAST WITH JESUS

Are you keeping watch for the dawn? Do you lie awake in the early morning watching the sun come up over trees and fields, houses, or walls?

In anthropology, that time of waiting is called liminality, from *limin*, meaning "threshold." It is the space you notice after starting your journey but before real change takes place. Your liminal space can be your best, calmest, and yet the most urgent time for prayer. Jesus chose his liminal spaces well—from the time of Lazarus' healing when he receded from his public face to spend time with his inner circle (at the beginning of his journey), to his walk to the cross. Whether in olive groves or mountainsides, or waiting for the dawn, Jesus spent ample time in prayer in the last months of his life, knowing he had come to a point of no return. Yet it was not quite time to culminate his mission.

Prayer can be your liminal space too, a time of watching and waiting for the dawn to come into your life. Photographers call the time between darkness and sunrise or sunset the "golden hour."

Some say it is the most beautiful hour of the day. Physicians call it the golden hour too, that liminal space between death and life in which someone can be saved. This morning, break your fast. Hold fast no longer to your past but wait for new life to begin anew with Jesus. Allow him to change you in the ways that he will. Feast with the Lord in your golden hour.

For breakfast, have a small bowl of oatmeal with fruits and a splash of honey or dash of cinnamon, along with a small glass of juice, a hot cup of coffee or tea, and a lot of prayer. As you wait for your coffee to brew, wait patiently for the Lord. You never know when the time will come that you will hear his voice, know his call, or see his face: "Keep watch. You don't know when your Lord will come." Just know that when he does, your life will change. Open your heart to that change.

Prayer

Lord, in the morning light, help me to spend time waiting and watching for your amazing grace. Amen.

LUNCH: "FIELD GREENS"

Have a lunch today of field greens topped with your favorite salad toppings, perhaps some mushrooms, nuts, artichokes, or beets, and drizzle with a bit of olive oil and balsamic. With it, have some water, iced tea, or lemonade.

The trees of the fields wave with joy because Jesus is coming to your house today.

Remember the story of Zacchaeus? He wanted to see Jesus so badly that he climbed a tree because the crowd was blocking his view. But we don't need to be satisfied with "seeing" Jesus from afar. No matter how insignificant we think we are or how mundane our lives, Jesus is never too "important" to spend time with any of us. Imagine today that you are looking out for Jesus in your life. Today is your day. Imagine him saying to you, "I need to come to your house today!" This lunch, imagine Jesus there dining with you. He is your house guest, and this time is set aside just for the two of you to get to know each other, to talk, to eat, to pray. Pray with him now.

Prayer

Lord, thank you for coming not just into my life, but into my home. I am so filled with joy to spend this time with you. Amen.

SUPPER: YOU ARE INVITED

"I have prepared a great feast! Everything is ready! Invite everyone you meet!"

Jesus has prepared a feast for you tonight. Are you "dressed" for dinner?

Remember the story of Mary and Martha. Both were invited to sit at the table with Jesus. But Martha was so concerned with details of hospitality, with getting the food just right, with setting the table just so, with fussing over cleaning the pots and maintaining decorum, that she didn't have time to sit at the table. When we get ready to go to a banquet, we so often think of bathing well, styling our hair, making sure our clothing is appropriate, and putting on our best decorum. Sometimes we can get so concerned with all of these trivialities that the "meal with friends" becomes more a show to get through than a relaxing and relational *selah*!

At the feast that Jesus prepares, he invites us not to "dress up" in our finest material things, but to "dress" ourselves with the cloak of grace. When we put on the dressings of authenticity, openness, transparency, and intimacy, we dress in the robes of relationship and show God that we are interested not in how to "put on" airs, but in the winds of the Spirit that God provides. Being "dressed" for the feast is to receive the gift of relationship, to come in gratitude and thanks to the table. For to Christ, it doesn't matter if you can afford gold or stones, or whether you dress in silk or burlap. God is interested only in the dressings of your heart and the sincerity of your presence. The ninth letter of the Greek alphabet is *iota* (intimacy, openness, transparency, intimacy). Dressing to the "nines" for Jesus' banquet means to come wearing only an "iota" of your means. Like Mary, tonight, be prepared to sit at the feet of Jesus, to revel in his grace, to realize that his interest in you is all about who you are, and nothing about how you cover it up. Unwrap the hindrances that bind you tonight and prepare to come to the banquet with Jesus.

In honor of you tonight, Jesus prepares for you a special dish that you may want to try cooking too: chicken curry with spinach.

Take some onion and only a small amount of curry powder and sauté them in olive oil. Season some chicken with salt and pepper and cook with the onions and curry in a pan until finished. Cook some spinach in oil tinged with pepper and coriander until wilted. Serve with the chicken, along with some mixed fresh olives and a glass of mint tea or sparkling water.

Prayer

Lord, allow me to be my most authentic self, to throw off the bulky clothing weighing me down, to cast off worries and doubt, and to sit at the feet of Jesus tonight, feasting on his power and grace. May I be filled with his love and nourished by his presence. Amen.

24 Days to Resurrection

BREAKFAST

As you wake, the world around you is coming alive. And as we move in our journey toward spring, the earth is coming alive too. It's the time of year that you look for signs of life. You notice on your walk to work that the tree branches have little nodules, buds waiting to break open. You notice that the corner market again has tulips, and soon they will sprout from gardens and flowerpots. You notice the difference in the feel of the wind, just a little bit warmer, with less of a chill. You notice that it's time to dig your garden, that the earth is less frozen, that you don't need your gloves. Can you read the weather too? Do you know at sunset what the morning will be like? Can you feel the direction of the wind?

What else do you notice? Do you notice the signs of life in others around you when you smile in parking lots, at bus stops, on the train, wanting to know what makes you feel so good? Do you notice the signs of life in yourself? So often we ask, as did many around Jesus, "Give me a sign so that I can really trust that you are the One, that you have power in my life to make it different, to make *me* different!" Are you looking for signs in all the wrong places? This morning, pay attention to the signs of Christ's presence in you and around you. Feel the signs of life as he stirs your heart and impassions your spirit. Feel his comfort, his love, his power, and his mercy wash over you like a fragrant shower. Bathe in the warmth of his grace. As you come to the table, know that Jesus is there. With fresh coffee or tea, juice from the vine, and a bowl of nuts and fruits, take a moment to feel the signs of life inside you. Toss in some cream and cardamom. It's time to feast with Jesus.

Prayer

Lord, help me to be aware of your presence even in the midst of a world that doubts and wants proof. Here in my time with you, I feel my life swell within me. And I smile. Amen.

LUNCH

On a beautiful day, you can hear the shouts and laughter of children running in the parks and playing in the streets. See their smiles, feel their energy, watch their glee, revel in their joy.

The kingdom of God belongs to those who are like children. Anyone who has children or grandchildren knows that children love to learn and discover new things. Whether delighting in the wiggle of a worm or feeling the wind propel them on a swing, whether staring with fascination at an ant or rolling down a hill, children love to spend time learning with and from others. They love to engage with someone who will teach them about the world and about God. Years ago, about this time of year, all elementary schools celebrated "field day." On field day, all of the children would spend the day outdoors, engaged together in all kinds of special games and team events. One of these I remember is the sack race. Children would be paired up together and given a burlap sack. You and your partner had to step into the sack and, holding it up together, needed to jump down the field together (in sync so that you wouldn't lose your balance) until you got to the end, and then you had to jump back again.

Life with Jesus is a little like that "sack dance." Imagine this lunchtime that sack game with Jesus. Step into your prayer space with Jesus beside you. Allow him to yoke with you arm in arm. Then gleefully and joyfully run through your day. Step and dance with him in sync and out. Enjoy your time with the Lord of Life. Laugh a little, shout a little, run out of breath a little. Best of all, know that if you fall down, he will lift you up again. Nourish your journey with joy. Take with you on your "field day" a wrap of some cheese, grain mustard, tomatoes, lettuce, some sprouts, and just a bit of oregano. And whatever you do, don't forget that Living Water.

Prayer

Lord, help me to enjoy life with you. Fill my time with you with laughter, joy, and energy. Amen.

SUPPER: A RECIPE FOR LOVE

"70 x 7." Why is it so hard sometimes to forgive? Why so hard for us to be joyful in God's mercy? Why is it so hard to love?

Are you a meal planner? Do you need everything to be just right and exactly and sufficiently measured in order to feel ok?

Is it hard sometimes to trust the Spirit and follow Jesus' "meal plan" for your life without plan or direction? How hard is it for you to do as Abraham did when God said simply, "Go to where I will lead you, and make no plan or provision"? For most of us, it's not easy. Peter, one of Jesus' closest disciples, had a very hard time letting go of his need for order, precision, and rules to follow. Remember when you heard him say, "Lord, when someone has sinned against me, how many times should I forgive him? Once? Twice? As many as seven times?" We too keep on wanting the "stuff" of our lives to be cut and dried and neatly wrapped up. But usually, life doesn't work that way.

Jesus tells us relationships are not simple. Relationships can't be built by following a recipe or calculating the price of butter. They can't be measured, fixed, or ruled. Love requires throwing all of our joys, our hurts, our experiences, and our dreams into the pot and letting things cook. Jesus reminds us that God does not care much about our rules and recipes but about the content of our love, the condition of our hearts.

At your table tonight, Jesus turns to you and says, "Relationships are messy. They don't make your life neat and tidy, orderly, or easy. They in fact can make things hard, chaotic, unpredictable, and emotional. You won't find a recipe for the "perfect relationship." But when people offer up the best parts of themselves, the results can be amazing.

Love, like relationships, doesn't need a reason to be. It just happens when you let go of rules and let Christ rule you.

Tonight, as you sit around your table, think about your relationship with Christ, your relationships with the people close to you, and the people you may not know well. The people you need to forgive. And the people you need to let in. Most of all, let Christ rule you. Tonight, put your recipes aside and celebrate the beautiful, complex, exquisite relationships in your life with a "stir fry" meal—a random blend of your pantry favorites. Try perhaps some cucumber, scallions, mushrooms, peppers, zucchini, snow peas, bean sprouts, or some lemongrass. Pour some olive oil or basil oil into your skillet. Add your ingredients along with some clove, fresh red chile, a bit of gingerroot, a little cornstarch and soy sauce, and a dash of sherry. If you want, add some shrimp to that and toss it up quickly. You can serve it over some rice laced with saffron or a bowl of couscous for your meal tonight. You could pair that with a side of carrot and mango salad topped with fresh chives. Try a dressing made of orange juice, lime juice, honey, and sesame seeds. And have a glass of cranberry juice on the side.

Prayer

Lord, help me to love the way you love—not by following rules or expectations, but by relishing every person in my life as a unique and unexpected gift. Amen.

24 Days to Resurrection

BREAKFAST: REDEEMING MARTHA

It's the dawn of Sabbath, and Jesus is out walking, journeying to see you, just as he journeyed to see his friends Mary, Martha, and Lazarus that day in Bethany. Can you see him coming?

Do you have the faith of Martha? When we think of faith, we most often think of Mary. We remember how busy Martha was that day when Jesus visited before. But today, Jesus encounters Martha first. She is the one who comes out to meet him, while Mary is much more engulfed in her grief. Martha's first words are, "Lord, if you had been with us, my brother would not have died." And when Jesus replies, "I am the resurrection and the source of all life. Everyone who lives and trusts in me will never truly die. Do you trust in this too?" Martha says immediately, "Yes, Lord. I believe that you are the Anointed One, God's own Son, who has come into this world." Only then does she bring Mary out. And Mary repeats Martha's first words before Jesus calls Lazarus from the tomb.

Do you have the faith of Martha? Even when things in your life seem to go wrong, do you know that Jesus has the power to overcome all adversity and even death in you and in others? Let your soul be revived this morning as you prepare to worship him with others. Whip together this morning a drink that will sustain you in body and spirit through the early part of the day. Take a blender and drop in a banana, some vanilla yogurt (refrigerated or frozen), a container of raspberries, a container of blackberries, a container of blueberries, and half a container of mango. Then add a bit of white grape juice or coconut water, some coconut milk if you like, a dash of cinnamon or cardamom or flax, and six ice cubes. Blend on high until smooth.

Prayer

Jesus, Lord of my Life, help me to know that when things don't go the way I hope they will, you will be there to lead me in a new and fresh direction. Help me to remember that you bring light from darkness, joy from grief, hope from despair, and most of all life from the stillness of death. Amen.

LUNCH: CATCHING A GLIMPSE

People were looking for Jesus, hoping to catch a glimpse of him in the city. All the while, some Jews were discussing him in the Temple.

Whether for or against him, everyone was talking about Jesus. Yet in our society today, there is a "hush" concerning talk about Jesus. No matter what anyone thinks, perhaps what we need most in our culture, in our churches, in our homes, is to start talking about Jesus again.

At lunchtime today, whether you are at home, in a restaurant, or visiting friends, what would it be like to strike up a conversation about Jesus and what he is doing in the world today?

Sometimes we talk about Jesus as though he is long gone and dead: old news. But if we truly have faith in the message of the gospel, have faith that Jesus is the resurrected Son of God, have faith that the Holy Spirit of Christ is living and active in this world, then we should have lots to talk about concerning Jesus. What is Jesus doing in your life? What is he doing in the lives of those around you?

Today for lunch, think hors d'oeuvres. Perhaps some mozzarella with tomato and basil drizzled with some balsamic and honey, some olives and cheese, or perhaps some fresh vegetables and fruits. Have a picnic feast. Look around you. Start the conversation. What if everyone was talking about Jesus?

Prayer

Lord, make me aware of your presence in my life today. Make me aware of you in every place and in every part of life. Amen.

SABBATH SUPPER

"You will be reborn as sons and daughters of the light."

This Sabbath evening, light some candles at your table. Tonight, imagine yourself at a long low table in the back room of an inn somewhere in the town of Bethany. Around the table are many people with you, including Jesus. On the table are many tallow candles. The wooden planks are strewn with multi-colored and designed linens, some with fringe. And around the table are placed large, tapestried pillows. A wine decanter sits in the center of the table, along with two large bowls, one filled with tandoori and karahi chicken, and the other with a yellow curry. Beside it is a small bowl of thin yogurt to mellow the spices of the food. On the floor is a large pitcher of water. Your glasses are filled and your bowls are ready. As all of you share the food, you look around at the flames of the candles flickering shadows upon the clay walls and upon the face of Jesus. In the pale light, his eyes shine dark and strong, kind, and yet powerful. He tells all of you, "If you have faith in me, if you know in your heart that I am *your* saving grace, your peace and passion, your connection to God, your messiah, then my light will illumine your heart in ways you cannot imagine."

Tonight, create dishes of passion and flame and light candles to the Lord. Feel the light of Christ in you.

Karahi Chicken: Heat olive or peanut oil in a hot wok or skillet. Add chopped onion and cook until golden. Stir in garam masala (this is a combination of roasted and ground spices, including 4 tbsps coriander seeds, 1 tbsp cumin seeds, 1 tbsp black peppercorns, 1 ½ tsps black cumin seeds [shahjeera], 1 ½ tsps dry ginger, ¾ tsp black cardamom [3–4 large pods approx.], ¾ tsp cloves, ¾ tsp cinnamon [2 x 1" pieces], and ¾ tsp crushed bay leaves), and add to that 1 tsp coriander, ½ tsp dried mint, and a bay leaf. Add to that diced chicken and cook 5–10 minutes. Add ¾ chicken stock and simmer for 10 minutes or more until the chicken is done. Stir in chopped cilantro.

Potato and Spinach Yellow Curry: Crush together some ginger, lemongrass, and coriander seeds. Stir the paste into heated oil, then stir in 2 tsps red curry paste and ½ tsp turmeric. Then add 1 cup of coconut milk and boil. Add potatoes and ½ cup of vegetable stock. Simmer for 15 minutes. When the potatoes are tender, stir in the spinach and simmer until wilted.

Prayer

Lord Jesus, fill my heart and soul with your everlasting light. Give me the passion to persevere in my faith, and may the flame of your Holy Spirit burn brightly in me so as to shine your light wherever I am. Amen.

Day Five
24 Days to Resurrection

BREAKFAST

Jesus told the Pharisees, "I have entered this world to announce a verdict that changes everything! Now those without sight may begin to see, and those who see may become blind."

Some of the Pharisees overhearing him said, "Surely we are not blind, are we?"

Jesus answered them, "If you were blind, you would be without sin. But because you claim you can see, your sin is ever present."

When you open your eyes in the morning, what is the first thing you see? In that place of half sleep, are you "seeing" with your physical eyes? Or is your mind "seeing" with its internal eye, its intuitive eye? In the dawn of your waking, do you "see" Jesus? Sometimes our physicality challenges our faith. Those who have no physical sight can tell you how much more intuitively they "feel" the world, hear sounds and intuit space, feelings, nuances of expression in voice and timbre, and even depth. Those with physical sight take much for granted. We rely on our eyes to "tell" us what is there and what is not. But do they tell us what is true?

The eyes that see Jesus the Messiah are not your physical eyes, but your perception and assurance of the great I AM! Do your physical eyes demand proof in your pudding? The more we "blind" ourselves to the false and superficial realities of our physical (worldly) sight, the more we can "see" God, feel God around us, and hear Christ's voice calling us. This is why we often close our eyes to pray, or why the dawn and dusk help us to see better.

This morning, can you see Christ as your Lord and Savior? Start your day today with some fruits and cheeses, perhaps cottage cheese and fruit if you wish, and coffee, tea, or a large glass of skim milk. Close your eyes and savor each taste and flavor. Experience the presence of Christ around you and within you.

Prayer

Lord, may I start each day with the freshness of your Spirit and the sight of your glory. Amen.

LUNCH

In this season of colds, viruses, and flus, many of us fear the transmission of these invisible germs through the touch of hands, especially the hands of little ones. Children seem always to have a runny nose or cough. Jesus overlooks all of this. In his time, people from all around brought their infants and children to Jesus hoping he would touch them in blessing. The disciples began admonishing them for doing this, but Jesus called out to the people instead and said, "No! Let these children come here to me. Never hold them back! Don't you realize the kingdom of God belongs to those who are like children? You can depend on this! If you don't receive the

Kingdom as a child would, you won't have a rat's tail chance of understanding how to enter into that kind of relationship with God!"

Jesus had the healing touch in so many ways. He touched people with far worse diseases than colds. This lunchtime, take some time to cherish your children, whether children, grandchildren, nieces, friends, or children you don't even know. Whether runny, dirty, food-strewn, or soggy, what beautiful and simple gifts to God they are in their simple willingness to come take the hand of Jesus. If only we could trust in him so easily.

This lunchtime, have a little fun. Be like a child and create a special sandwich. Use the cookie cutter of your choice to make a specially shaped sandwich. You can use some tuna, mayo, and perhaps some herbs. Or perhaps you can create some little sandwiches with cucumber and cream cheese. Complement your sandwich with a side of celery and a glass of juice.

Prayer

Lord, feasting with you is like a run in the sun. May this break in my day remind me of the joy of living in you. Amen.

SUPPER: GO FISH

Jesus had very good reasons for calling several fishermen to be in discipleship with him. Have you ever gone fishing? If you have, you know that whether standing knee-deep fly-fishing or sitting in a boat on the water, while enjoyable, this favorite pastime can also take a lot of patience, endurance, and time, and it can be quite challenging. Even more so for a fisher who derives his or her life sustenance from fishing. In Jesus' day, fishermen would spend days on the sea sometimes, sitting and casting their nets with nothing to show for it. They persevered through all kinds of storms, endured all kinds of hardships, tossed to and fro on little boats, and spent many a slow day with only patience and hope that they would stumble upon the right place and the right time that would yield a net full of fish. And when they did, they took everything that came into the net. Sometimes they might catch some very strange creatures, other times, only some small minnows. But whatever came to them, they were thankful for, and they worked together to haul in the net. Then the next day, they went back out again. They didn't fear failure. They knew that in order to find plentiful fish just at the right place and right time, they needed to be out on the sea, watching and waiting, casting and adventuring.

To be "fishers" of people takes patience too. You can't decide and discern which fish will come into the net. You take them all, and you love them all. You sail the seas, and you swim with the seafood. How do you know when you are in the right place at the right time to save a life for Jesus? How do you know when the time is ripe? You don't. But if you don't go out and sail the seas, splashing among the fish, you will never be that saving grace for someone who really needs to come ashore. Jesus' fishers are lifesavers, not life takers. Their rugged hands are filled with grace. Tonight, as you savor your fish, remember the people in your life who cast nets in your life. Who taught you to pray, caught your attention, sought your life, brought you to Jesus? Who were your fishers? And for whom will you be that fisher too?

Tonight, prepare a dish of Cod Mediterranean. Make a sauce of chopped tomatoes, tomato paste, capers, olives, and pepper and heat it slowly in a pan. Place your fish in a casserole dish topped with bay leaf, peppercorns, lemon rind, and onions. Bake for 25 minutes. Top with the sauce, some parsley, and lemon. Then lay a platter filled with some fresh broccoli, celery, carrot sticks, corn cobs, and red cabbage. Make a hummus dip of eggplant, roasted sesame seeds, a small bit of sesame oil, lime rind, shallots, a dash of red chile, and a pinch of sugar. On the side, fill a glass of vegetable juice tossed with a splash of hot sauce and a glass of fresh water.

Prayer

Lord Jesus, let my hands be your hands, my eyes be your eyes, my life be your life. Give me the heart and mind of a fisherman and a soul filled with your grace. Amen.

24 Days to Resurrection

BREAKFAST

"May my prayer be set before you like incense." (Psalm 141:2).

"For we are to God the pleasing aroma of Christ" (2 Corinthians 2:15).

This morning, resurrect your senses as you wake with the sound of rain on your windows and roof, the smell of fresh coffee or tea, and the scent of your favorite oils or incense. Fragrant incense in Jesus' day was made from natural ingredients from plants and tree resins. Based in olive oil, the most prominent oil of the region (olive trees abounded everywhere), favorites were added, such as frankincense, galbanum, myrrh, cinnamon, cane, cassia, henna, spikenard, saffron, tea tree oil, algum (sandalwood), balsam, coriander, mint, myrtle, and others. The aromatic mixture was used often during prayer. People felt that the burning of these incenses signified the sweet fragrance of their prayers rising up to God. Our prayers are a sweet-smelling gift to God, an offering of the fragrance of our love. As you sit at the table with Jesus, smell the aromas around you, and awaken your tastes to the intricate flavors of aromatic fruits as you offer up your morning prayers to him.

This morning, arrange some melon, watermelon, guavas, nectarines, mango, and berries in your bowl or plate. Top with some shredded coconut, mint leaves, or rose petals. On the side, place some yogurt mixed with cinnamon, cardamom, clove, and some orange and lime juices. Add a slice of cassia bark for good measure. Or heat some sugar, water, and your aromatic spices in a pan just to simmer and pour over your fruit. Top with mint. As you eat your aromatic fruit, sipping your freshly ground coffee, perhaps adding a slice of whole-grain seeded toast, may your body, mind, and soul be a prayer to the Lord.

Prayer

Lord, fill me with the fragrance of your love. Let the aromas of these prayers to you linger around me through the day to remind me of this time with you. Amen.

LUNCH: LET IT RAIN

"You heavens above, rain down my righteousness; let the clouds shower it down. Let the earth open wide, let salvation spring up, / let righteousness flourish with it; I, the LORD, have created it" (Isaiah 45:8).

This is the season of rain, when the Lord opens the floodgates of heaven and rains down upon us his glory, his amazing grace, the salvation of his Son. And the Lord's rain falls on all people Matthew 5:45).

When it rains, the earth bears its fruit, and all creation sings the song of the Lord. Did you ever notice how in the rain, sounds echo differently in the air? They become more vivid, amplified. The sounds resonate in the water within the atmosphere. This is what it is like when God's love rains down upon us. Suddenly, the world grows more lovely and vivid, and God's voice resonates in the air. You may have heard the expression, "Love is in the air." When God rains down the righteousness of Christ, "love" is in the air. The Spirit of Christ is around you, with you, and within you. Let the drops of his magnificent love fall upon your shoulders like the rain, washing you, exhilarating you, lifting you, nourishing you. Let that love take root in your heart and rise up within you. And may everyone around you be blessed with the nourishment of your spirit.

This lunchtime, make a fragrant soup, for you are a fragrance of love to others today. Slice some lemongrass and add 2 cups of coconut milk, lime leaves, and ginger, and then boil. Add some water, strips of chicken, mushrooms, and basil. Simmer until tender. Then stir in 3 chilis, a splash of lime juice, and cilantro, and serve fresh. Add a side of fruits of the field to remind you of the love you are to others. Don't forget your Living Water.

Prayer

Lord, rain down on me today the blessings of your Holy Spirit. Infuse in me the freshness of your love and grace. Amen.

SUPPER

The weeks before Passover were in Jesus' day, and still are, times of preparation. Part of that preparation included the teaching of children and others about how to answer what is called the "four ques-tions." These four questions make sure that children know why the ritual is done and how it relates to the story of God and the Jewish people. During the Passover ritual, the story is told, and the ques-tions then are presented to the children around the table to make sure they understand the significance of the meal and their role in carrying forward the faith. As you journey toward resurrection with Jesus, can you think about the story of Christ's sacrifice and resurrec-tion and your celebration of his salvation for your life? What ques-tions would you ask your children? What questions would you ask yourself? Can you see yourself in Christ's story of Life?

Are you thinking about preparing yourself for your resurrection life? Jesus spent the last three weeks before his ordeal tucked away with his disciples for the most part. He withdrew from public minis-try and spent part of his time in intimate relationship and teaching. He meant to prepare his flock for the mission he needed to fulfill, to make sure they understood what it would mean for the redemption of humanity and all of God's creation. As they spent those last weeks together, they spent lots of time asking questions, struggling with their faith, and sharing time together around the table. Tonight, as you prepare your life for Christ, what questions do you have to ask Jesus? What do you struggle with in your faith? Jesus is there to talk with you and walk with you through these last weeks of your journey together.

For this time with him tonight, prepare a dish of ground lamb with peas. (If you do not like lamb, you may substitute ground beef.) Heat some oil in a pan and brown onion slices. Add red chiles, cilan-tro, and chopped tomatoes. Simmer for a while. Add some ginger, chili powder, and cinnamon to the mixture. Then stir in the ground lamb or beef and brown it for 10 minutes. Add peas last to the pan and cook until done, approximately 8 more minutes. Serve topped with bits of cilantro.

You can complement this dish with a side of Fragrant Coconut Rice: Heat ginger, cloves, lemongrass, nutmeg, cinnamon, bay leaf, lime rind, creamed coconut, and water in a large pan to a boil. You will need about 2 cups of water. Add 1 ¾ cups of basmati rice. (You can add some saffron if you choose as well.) Heat for approximately 15 minutes until the rice is tender. Before serving, pepper it to taste and serve it with your lamb dish.

Prayer

Lord, prepare me for your love and mercy. Prepare my heart in faith. Prepare my life in mission. Prepare my soul to reach only and ever for you. Amen.

24 Days to Resurrection

BREAKFAST: "THIS ISN'T ABOUT WHAT YOU DESERVE."

You have a place at the table. Imagine today going to visit Jesus where he has put aside rooms for a feast. You see a large wooden door, and when you enter it, a long table is set with many places. You wander in, seeing others beginning to gather and take seats. You wonder if there will be room for you, if you should have called first, whether you belong. After all, you didn't let him know you were coming.

As the room fills with people, you stand and watch, not knowing what to do. Just then, you see Jesus standing to the side of the table, and he is motioning for you to come. Shyly, you move toward him. He is smiling at you. You try to say, "I'm sorry I am here at a bad time." But Jesus tells you, "No, I am expecting you. Here is your seat."

"My seat?" you ask. "But I have no reservation, no right to be here."

Jesus leads you to a seat and tells you to sit and eat with him. He says to you, "This is your seat at my table, whenever you come here. You are not a passerby. You are always my treasured guest."

This morning, Jesus has a feast for you, a special treat, and a special blessing. Join him in his celebration of life. Set before you today is a breakfast of dates, figs, and dried grapes (currants in Jesus' day were something like raisins) in almond milk, with a side plate of cheeses and coffee. A very special dish is prepared especially for you: warm currants in cassis that was prepared by heating a cup or more of currants with 4 tbsp of sugar and the rind and juice of an orange. After boiling, strain the currants and return the juice to the pan. Add 2 tsp arrowroot and a little water and boil, then add 2 tbsp crème de cassis. Pour back over the currants and top with mascarpone or whipped cream. Top with a sprig of mint.

Enjoy your meal and revel this morning in the gift of Christ's love and feast.

Prayer

Lord, your grace overwhelms me with gratitude. "You set a table before me, and my cup overflows." How do I deserve such a gift from you? May my heart ever be in your care and service. Amen.

LUNCH: "REMEMBER, WHAT IS HUMANLY IMPOSSIBLE IS POSSIBLE WITH GOD."

No one is perfect. Nor can we be. Jesus' disciples were used to doing all kinds of things and following all kinds of rules in order to be "good enough" for God. One man tried very hard to impress Jesus with how well he followed every rule. He asked Jesus, "Good teacher, what do I need to do to inherit the life of the age to come?" He was hoping for a response of praise. But Jesus caught on to him right away and saw his concept of obedience and reward in his word "good." And he challenged him, "Why did you just call me good? No one is good but God. Only God." Then Jesus proceeded to tell him, "You know what the Hebrew scriptures tell you to do, but you can still do more." And Jesus challenged him to give everything up and to follow as a disciple with him. At that, the man's pride was shot down, and he worried that he had not achieved salvation; for he believed that he needed to measure up to "earn" God's blessing.

Jesus used this as a lesson to his other disciples, saying, "It would be easier for a camel to squeeze through the narrow gates of Jerusalem than for a 'rich' person to enter God's garden." The others, still muddled by the concept of salvation by good works, said, "Then how can anyone be good enough to be saved?" Jesus answered, "No one can. But remember, …what is humanly impossible is possible with God."

No one is good enough. Not you. Not the best disciple in the world or by the law's standards. God is not about laws; God is about love. Your salvation is not about how good you are or how much good you have accomplished, but about your relationship with God. When you realize how much you have fallen short and how much you have missed the mark in your life, it is in that moment of humility, that God will lift you up. Jesus said, "I am the Way, the Truth, and the Life . Come along with me. Be my disciple. Sit with me for a while and learn the truth about God and about salvation. Stop worrying about what you must do. Come dine with me instead. Don't you know who I am?"

This lunchtime, spend some time in prayer with Jesus. Tell him where you have failed, where you have fallen short, and that your life needs him to be fulfilled. Today, trade in everything that is possible, everything you can do on your own, and nourish yourself instead with God's "impossible" gift of grace.

Today, create a salad made from the best of God's creation. On your greens, toss some cherry tomatoes, soft cheese, bunches of chives and basil, some peppered bits of steak or roasted chicken, and a shake of Greek seasoning. Top it with your favorite olive oil and a splash of red wine vinegar. Dream an impossible dream.

Prayer

Lord, may my life be made perfect only in you. Give me rest from my urges to make things "good" for myself. Give me the faith to know that when I am with you, I am already everything I need to be. And that "Christ in me" is more than good. It is beautiful. Amen.

SUPPER: "IT MUST NOT BE SO AMONG YOU."

Why is it so hard to have faith? We would rather have the handbook called "12 Easy Ways to Achieve Salvation" or have someone tell us that if we only do this, that, and the other thing, we'll have it all. The world operates in terms of success, achievement, competition, and attainment. But with Jesus, all of those things are hindrances to faith and love. Love does not compete. Faith cannot be achieved. Those of us who grew up on *Star Wars* movies remember well the conversation between Luke Skywalker and Yoda as Yoda trains Luke to serve as a Jedi. Luke says, "I'll try." Yoda replies, "There is no try."

"What do you fear to lose?" Jesus asks you. Look at your hands. What are you holding on to? At the end of your day, what will you most value? Scoop up a handful of sand. Now let it run slowly through your fingers. What you attain or seek to control is as those grains of sand. You may grip something you seek to control in your hand for a while, but the moment you open your fist, it all slips away like granules in a cloud of dust. It is hard to live a "fisted" life. Now put your hands instead in the hands of another. Entwine your fingers together. I guarantee that when you open your hands again, you will always feel that touch. It takes a lot of faith to live with an open hand, a hand that reaches out instead of clenches. "Stop trying to hold in your hands what was never meant to be yours," Jesus says. Open hand, open heart. Reach out and touch, and your heart will know trust.

Tonight, finger food is what Jesus shares with you, a plate of raw vegetables and some stuffed tomatoes and peppers (fill them perhaps with cream cheese and chives or with tuna salad, or a mixture of cheese like ricotta, and meat or rice). Add some smoked salmon and a variety of fresh whole fruits. As Jesus shares this meal with you, share yours with someone too. Feed someone across the table from you and let them feed you. Use your hands in service. Close your eyes in faith. Make your meal a feast of love.

Prayer

Lord Jesus, use my hands. Make them an extension of a heart that trusts and a faith in you that flourishes and endures. Amen.

24 Days to Resurrection

BREAKFAST: "EVERYONE ATE AND WAS SATISFIED."

A mouthful of truth and a cup filled with blessing—every feast time with the Lord restores your soul and fills you with the Bread that does not go stale and Living Water enough to keep you in an everlasting celebration of life.

Life with Jesus is a mountaintop experience, just as it was for so many on that mountaintop in Galilee so many years ago. One of the last times Jesus was among the public, people followed him around for three days, even to the top of the mountain, because he was healing so many.

First Peter talks of the faith of unspeakable joy, a faith so strong that it takes one's breath away, gratitude so magnificent that it can't be spoken. If Jesus the healer was a handful, the joy of faith in Jesus was quite a mouthful! Are you hungry for something in your life? Is there a part of you that remains unhealed? Have you experienced the joy that cannot be contained? This morning, let Jesus fill you with unspeakable joy and unrestrained passion, and faith unfailing. As you sit at the table with the Lord this morning, feel his hand upon you, healing all of the doubt and worry within you, healing you in body and soul, lifting you in peace and joy. Feel him take your hand. Feel the ruggedness of his fingers, the gentleness of his touch, the strength of his grasp. Let your whole heart be filled with unspeakable joy. Let your faith rise within you. As you share your meal with him, let Jesus feed your soul. Let each bite fill you with the knowledge that Jesus is your life.

Let today be a day of whole grain cereal topped with fresh whole fruits. Add a bit of skim milk or a touch of cream. Add a side of juice, and your stomach—-as well as your soul-will be filled and content throughout your day.

Prayer

Lord, fill me with your great blessings. May my heart and soul know no hunger, and may my faith know no boundary. Amen.

LUNCH: MOST WANTED: "BLESSED IS EVERYONE WHO WILL EAT BREAD IN THE KINGDOM OF GOD!"

Jesus is not merely about feeding those who don't have food. He is about feeding those who want to eat with him, feeding them with the rich bread of heaven. Do you want to break bread with Jesus?

One day, Jesus told a group of scholars the story of a man who hosted a huge banquet. He had invited a huge amount of guests, all

who partied with him when times were good, and all who agreed to come now. But when the time came for the feast, they made all kinds of excuses not to be there. Either they were busy, they were suddenly elsewhere engaged, something came up, or they needed to do something else with someone else instead. (They were fickle friends, and they were afraid or shy to be seen with him.) The Master knew these were excuses, and so he went out and invited all those who were hungry and grateful to come instead, anyone from the fields and streets whom he had encountered on his travels, all those unafraid to be seen with him, unconcerned, even honored, to be known as his companions and guests. No one on the original guest list came. But the room was filled with others who did.

Will you bear the name of Jesus on your guest list? Will you bear the scandal of attending the dinner of the one "Most Wanted" by the authorities that you must face and live with every day? In our society, are you ashamed or proud to be seen dining with Jesus? To let people know he is residing with you at your home? Are you one of those who "most want" to be in relationship with the Lord and to share with him the bread of his kingdom?

For lunch this day, make it a sandwich day. Take the bread of your choice and create a sandwich with your favorite things inside. Mine is a BLT: bacon, lettuce, and tomatoes. Drink a side of vegetable juice and top it off with a piece of fruit for a luncheon feast to share with Jesus.

Prayer

Lord, let the attitudes and cynicisms of this world about you pass by me unnoticed. Make me always a worthy guest at your table and a grateful receiver of your grace. Amen.

SUPPER: "FLAVORLESS SALT IS ABSOLUTELY WORTHLESS."

Do you like to spice things up? Today, we have a number of seasonings to add to our food, but nothing beats salt.

Salt in Jesus' day was a very important ingredient, not only for seasoning but also for healing, preserving, purifying, burning, and livening things up. Salt was used in every Temple and table offering. "Season all your grain offerings with salt," says Leviticus 2:13. Whenever you shared a meal at the table, you were to use salt. For a sacrifice to be acceptable to God, it had to be salted. Therefore, as those who sacrifice their lives in discipleship to Jesus, we must be salted with the compassion and gratitude of our Lord's amazing sacrifice and salted with the grace that sends us into the world to offer up living food to those in need of Jesus.

Salt can symbolize tears, like the tears that Jesus shed for Jerusalem and for the sin of humanity. When we sit down to feast with Jesus, we become part of the living sacrifice and part of the living bread that revives, flavors, and feeds others.

But there is an even more important symbol for salt. Leviticus 2:13 refers to God's covenant with humanity as a covenant of salt. It was a covenant that was incorruptible, unbreakable, passionate, and seasoned with love. Salt stood for permanence (the way meat could be preserved), as the covenant between humanity and God is permanent. Salt also purifies. Humans are by nature often lacking in spiritual purity; therefore, our sacrifice in the form of a meal taken together should be seasoned with salt, as we must be ourselves seasoned by Christ. Christ seasons within us the grace and passion that

defines our lives as disciples and reveals the way we "taste" to others who encounter us.

Throughout history, people have confirmed their agreements with God, have seasoned their meals with prayer, have added to their breaking of bread with faithful and loving conversation. Each time we eat and drink together with Christ at our table, we "taste" and "temper" together the salt of our discipleship. A "covenant of salt" signified an everlasting covenant. A "salty discipleship" signifies an everlasting relationship with the Lord Jesus in your life and at your table. Tonight, make your table your altar. Make it a special night in which you offer up a savory steak as you savor your covenant with God.

Heat a skillet to very hot with a small bit of oil. Then brown some small fillet steaks. Make sure to salt and pepper them well on each side. After browning a few minutes on each side, reduce the heat and cover with foil. Cook 5–8 minutes until done to preference. Serve with a balsamic drizzle and a garnish of parsley. With it, toss some asparagus into a glass baking dish or onto a cookie sheet. Roll in a small bit of olive oil, and then season with salt and lemon pepper. Bake at 400 degrees for 10 minutes. Serve with a mozzarella salad, made up of a bed of spinach topped with watercress, salted tomatoes, mozzarella, and some balsamic mixed with honey and oil. Don't forget your living water.

Prayer

Lord, give me a salty faith. May my life be a living covenant to all who encounter me, that when they see me, they see you. Amen.

24 Days to Resurrection

BREAKFAST: ALL PUFFED UP— "BANANA SOUFFLE"

A formerly blind man whose sight was restored by Jesus spoke to the Pharisees berating him for following Jesus: "This man must come from God. Otherwise, this miracle would not be possible. Only God can do such things." The Pharisees answered, "You were born under a cloud of sin. How can you, of all people, lecture us?" Then they banished him from their presence. But Jesus went after him.

The Pharisees were so full of themselves, they had no room in their hearts for Jesus to fill. They felt that they were special because they knew and followed Moses' law to perfection. Their rules for keeping others out didn't exclude them from attacking those not as "good" as they felt they were, like wolves in a sheep's pen. (A wolf in sheep's clothing is worse than a wolf itself. That wolf doesn't pretend to be someone else.) While the Pharisees were all "puffed up" with pride—pride that would make them haughty and angry enough to want to get rid of Jesus so he couldn't show them up—Jesus filled his followers with the healing and wholeness that would allow them to rise up and be at one with God.

This morning, let yourself be filled with that healing spirit too. Know that no matter how much the world "inflates" itself in all kinds of ways, only in Jesus will you be lifted, will you rise up to fly above all worry and doubt, will you feel the heaviness of the world slip away from you and know the lightness and the buoyancy of the Holy Spirit within you.

To celebrate this time with Jesus this morning, create a banana soufflé. Watch the heaviness of a banana rise up and become the lightest of breakfasts. May this metaphor stay with you throughout the day to remind you of the way your life will change in Jesus.

Preheat your oven to 450 degrees. Brush ramekin dishes with oil. Cut banana into bits and place in a blender with a tbsp of lime juice and a tbsp of coconut milk. Blend until smooth. Add 4 egg yolks and a tsp of sugar and blend until smooth again. In another bowl, combine the egg whites and whisk until stiff. Whisk in ¼ cup of sugar until glossy. Fold the egg white into the banana mixture gently and spoon it into the dishes. Bake for 8 minutes or until well risen and golden. Serve up immediately.

Prayer

Lord, raise me up to be a loyal follower of you. Let all worries fall away, and let me feel the lightness of your yoke upon me. Amen.

LUNCH: GOING OUT TO PASTURE

For this lunch, make it a "field" day with Jesus. Create a green leafy salad with as many types of leaves and flowers as you can find. Do you have some of these in your yard? Perhaps some frisée, oakleaf lettuce, radicchio, chicory, arugula, basil, parsley, or edible flowers. You could also find some chives and fresh dandelion and other herbs to strew within. Top with a dash of salt and some Herbs de Provence. Add a bit of sheep or goat cheese for good measure, and you don't even need a dressing.

When I was young, children used to spend a lot of time outdoors. Many of our meals came right from the yard: dandelion with rich bacon dressing (you need to pick it before the blooms appear to keep its sweet flavor), fresh picked peas in warm milk, mint tea cooked on the stove and iced (once you plant mint, it will grow forever!), garden lettuce, carrots, tomatoes, and herbs. Fruits from the trees. Berries from the fields. But what we kids loved the most was to sit on a nearby little hill, relaxing, watching the others at play, and chewing on bits of "onion grass." It grew right in the midst of the grassy slopes. Like handfuls of chives, onion grass gave off a mild oniony flavor. Content to be outdoors for whole days at a time, playing and enjoying the breeze, when dusk settled in, we would rise up and scatter at the voices of parents calling out the doors, "It's time to come in!" Dirt embedded in our feet and soaked in the scents of the outdoor air, we would scamper into our houses, sink into warm baths, wash away the day, and settle in for the night. Tomorrow would be another day "in the field." Every one of us was given the freedom to roam the yards and fields during the day, as long as we followed our parents' voices back home at night.

Free will is one of the most beautiful gifts God gives us. As followers of Jesus, we are free (and encouraged) to roam the fields by day, to eat from the vines and play among the branches; to talk among ourselves and to explore the paths and byways of the world. But when his voice calls us—whether back from a precipice or to follow him down a right path, whether to come in from the rain or to gather in for the night—we come. Jesus tells us that the sheep are safe from harm as long as they follow him and that every one of them will know his voice: "I know my sheep, and my sheep know me. There are many more sheep than you can see here, and I will bring them as well. They will hear my voice, and the flock will be united. One flock. One shepherd."

Sometimes we can wander far away. Sometimes we can get lost in the tangles of sin or in the confusion of the world's many streets and open doors. If ever you are lost, just listen for the voice of Jesus. He is here in your house, in your place, at your table, and he is calling you home.

Prayer

Lord, let me enjoy the bounty of your fields and the richness of your love. Let me always listen for your voice that will always keep me safe. Hold me close, Lord. Take me home. Amen.

SUPPER

"My life cannot be taken away by anybody else. I am giving it of my own free will. My authority allows me to give my life and to take it up again. All this has been commanded by my Father."

The salmon is a very unusual fish. It spends half of its life in fresh water and half in salt water. The salmon is born in the river, then swims to the sea for most of its adult life. But when it's time to spawn, it returns to the river, to its natal place. It has an uncanny ability to smell its way home. The salmon run upriver is exhausting for the salmon, which needs to swim miles upstream through strong currents and rapids. It leaps over waterfalls and navigates through rocks and dams to reach its destination. And it doesn't stop even to eat during this time. At last, it reaches home and lays its eggs. Most salmon die after this. If they do not, they return to the ocean to do it all over again.

When I think of the early Christian symbol the *ichthys*, I can't help but think of the salmon—and the apostles. No matter what our early followers of Jesus had to go through, they were determined to go out and live out the gospel within the world, telling others about the precious gift of our Lord. At the end of the day or week, they would always return home—to the church, their gathering place, where they found their "home" with Jesus. Gathering around the table, they would break bread with the Master, singing praises to his glorious name. Here they would "spawn" new disciples, helping them to learn to "swim" out their newly consecrated baptisms in a world that could be hard, dangerous, exhausting, and without reward. They never gave up. They never gave in. And they identified themselves with the sign of the *ichthys*—Jesus Christ, Son of God and Savior!

Whenever you find yourself exhausted from this world, feeling that you are swimming upstream and not getting anywhere, and the navigation is hard and the road is long—remember, Jesus is swimming beside you, giving you strength, breath, endurance, and hope. And when you reach home, he will be waiting for you. As you make your way through this world, living and loving, passing the covenant of Christ on to others, making disciples, telling the stories of Jesus to the next generations, know that Jesus is right there at the table with you, and all the others with him are the church. All are nodding and saying, "You have made him glad!"

For dinner tonight, celebrate your life's journey with a salmon fillet, seasoned only with olive oil and a pinch of lemon pepper. Enjoy it with some steamed broccoli topped with cheese and lemon and lots of Living Water.

Prayer

Lord, my life is a living sacrifice to you. Make me an able servant, a strong conveyor of the gospel, a hardy and passionate disciple of the faith. Amen.

24 Days to Resurrection

BREAKFAST: "TEACH US TO PRAY."

The prayer Jesus taught his disciples begins with an acknowledgment of the Lord's great holiness. Then it asks that God's kingdom might come to pass within our lives—a time in which God and all of creation and humanity are reunited with God in love and wholeness. The prayer asks for our daily sustenance and nourishment, the kind that only God can give—for our physical as well as our emotional and spiritual needs. It asks for forgiveness for the times we have failed, and protection from the temptations that would cause us to fall away from God's loving arms again. In sum, the prayer acknowledges God's great power and ability to help us to come into (and stay in) relationship with the one God who makes us whole and gives us our life. It asks that we be united, asks that we stay united, asks that we be continually reunited if and when we falter, and asks that God do everything to keep us from breaking that union. This prayer is a powerful prayer.

So often in our lives, we look to prayer not as a surrender but as a secret formula for getting what we want. Rather than an acknowledgment and seeking of the power of God to take our lives and make them whole, we want our prayers to be "spells" to get God to alter life to the way we want it to be instead. When God fails to do our wishes and desires in the way we feel God should, we turn away, and we claim God can't possibly love us enough.

The Lord's Prayer acknowledges God's amazing and powerful love, a love that does not grant us in our limited view what we think we should have, but what we really most need. For when the Lord is in our life, all our needs will be fulfilled—perhaps not in the way we thought, but in bigger and even better ways than that.

This morning, have a whole grain "power" breakfast with fruit and juice. And celebrate God's power in your life.

Prayer

Lord, your will and not mine, your path and not my own. For your love is greater than the life I know. May I seek instead the eternal life that is in you. Amen.

LUNCH: BIDING TIME

In the Gospel of John, the writer moves quickly from the Feast of Dedication when Jesus is teaching in the Jerusalem Temple (December) to six days before the Passover Feast (March/April), when he is about to return to Jerusalem in the procession that would lead that week to his death. Already at the Feast of Dedication, some were trying to stone him for saying he was the Son of God. From that point on, Jesus goes "on the lam." When he leaves Jerusalem that December, he will spend some time near the Jordan River, the origin of his mission, where he had originally been baptized by John. The people of that region will follow him everywhere he goes. As his notoriety increases, he needs to be careful where he travels and stays, so as to avoid those wanting to kill him. He spends most of his time along the river in the region of Nazareth, staying away from the Temple until things die down a bit. At the end of February, he will linger two days after receiving the news about Lazarus, so that no one can try to entrap him, as they know he will go to Bethany for his friend's final days.

After the raising of Lazarus, news got out to the chief priests and Pharisees about Jesus' location and what he had done, and they called a council meeting to talk about what to do. The people were rallying around Jesus more and more, and the authorities began to truly be afraid of what could happen next. Temple officials feared that the Romans would think they were not keeping their word to them. What if the Romans thought the people were going to revolt? And what if they decided it was better to destroy the Temple? Temple authorities were all about keeping things the same, and Jesus was about making the world different. And to them, "different" was threatening. It was then that their decision was firm. They needed somehow to have Jesus executed. Knowing this, until the time was right, Jesus refrained from walking publicly among the people in Judea.

As many already were making the journey to Jerusalem early to prepare for the Passover, which would begin at the end of next week, Jesus hid in the town of Ephraim. "The chief priests ordered that if anyone knew the whereabouts of Jesus of Nazareth, it must be reported immediately, so that they could arrest him." But the people of Ephraim protected him. Jesus would stay hidden away all of the next week, right up until he would make his way back to Lazarus' home for the last time in Bethany near Judea, the time of his final anointing. From there, he would make his way to Jerusalem, and his week of "reckoning" would commence.

Now one week still in our journey with Christ before he makes that final trip to Judea, Jesus is biding time. To "bide time" is to engage in a period of waiting—for the right moment to come to do something important or momentous. But he is not waiting alone. You are there with him, you and the disciples closest to him in this time. Ephraim was the name for the Palestinian town now called Taybeh, a lone Christian town northeast of Jerusalem. It overlooks the wilderness, the Jordan Valley, Jericho, and the Dead Sea. The symbol of the town is the pomegranate, named for the fruit that Jesus used in one of his parables there. In that village, Jesus gathered with those closest to him, preparing them for his final mission with teaching and praying. The disciples and Jesus likely feasted on those pomegranates, among the dishes prepared for them there, as they spent time together in prayer.

Today, make this luncheon time a time for prayer with Jesus. Prepare a dish of marinated eggplant, fresh with a salsa made with pomegranate.

Roast sliced eggplant in the oven for 45 minutes. Then prepare a salsa of walnuts, cider vinegar, cloves, chilis, walnut oil, parsley, coriander, and salt. Top it with slices of fried goat cheese and pomegranate seeds. With it, have a licorice root tea. Bide some time with Jesus.

Prayer

Lord, help me to face each season in life biding my time in prayer. For I want to face every decision and every obstacle with you by my side. Amen.

SUPPER: "YOU ARE A LIVING STONE."

A temple is a place of strength, learning, sacrifice, prayer, and praise. And you are part of Christ's spiritual temple. You, in your very bones, were made for praise and worship. When you sing your praises to Christ, you will feel the joy of the Lord resonating through skin and marrow.

Tonight, as you spend some time with Jesus, find a stone. Hold it in your hand. Feel its smooth, hard strength, its substance in your palm. Feel it getting warm as you clench your fist around it. Now hold it to your cheek. Can you feel the heat? The love of Christ in you is like that stone. When you put your hand in the hand of another, he or she will feel the power of Christ resonating through you, feel the warmth of his touch, feel the substance of his presence. You are a living stone of Christ's temple and a building block of his kingdom. Stones not only build temples; they build bridges too. They are the foundations for relationships and the means for footpaths, the stones of faith and the stones of love.

Tonight, create kabobs of meatballs or beef, peppers, onions, tomatoes, and zucchini. Roast them over a fire or in your oven. Top with some Greek seasoning. Enjoy with a bottle of sparkling water.

Prayer

Lord, make me a part of your kingdom. Create in me a solid faith, that I may stand tall in the face of adversity and build bridges of love over every pass. Amen.

24 Days to Resurrection

BREAKFAST: "CAN YOU DRINK FROM MY CUP?" SMOOTHIES

This morning, make a smoothie to start your day: a banana, fresh fruit of your choice, some guava juice, fruit sorbet, coconut milk, and a bit of ice. Blend together well for a refreshing start this Sabbath day.

As you sip together with Jesus this morning, and you express your desire to follow him, he asks you, "Can you drink from my cup?" Jesus explains that the kingdom of God is not about being in the best place but being willing to follow him into the worst. Jesus knows that the road ahead will be hard. And it will be a hard road for his disciples to follow if they see the world in terms of the way everyone else does. He needs you to see differently. Once you do, he knows that you will look different to others. Can you handle looking "different" in the world? Can you keep your eyes straight when others look at you sideways? Jesus' cup is the cup of transformation. When you drink it, it will change you from the inside out.

Jesus' cup is not just a cup of blessing but a cup of blood – the kind that binds people together. When children are young, they sometimes vow to become "blood sisters or blood brothers." They prick their fingers and mingle their blood together in a bond that says they will stand by each other to the end. Jesus asks you, "Can you be that for me? With me? Will you share my cup?" These are hard questions. This morning, as you pick up your cup, will you take Jesus' hand and pledge yourself to him for life?

Prayer

Lord, make me a disciple of the "cup"—a follower of your path and a lover of your people. Amen.

LUNCH: DON'T THINK SKIM WHEN YOU CAN HAVE WHOLE

Often, when it came to understanding Jesus, the disciples were a few peas short of a casserole. They were used to thinking literally, and Jesus spoke in metaphors that required a bit more depth.

One day, after the Pharisees and Sadducees had spent some time in a verbal duel with Jesus, trying to trip him up, Jesus wanted to explain to his disciples something about the nature of these pompous scholars.

Now the disciples had just come across the Sea of Galilee to meet Jesus, and when they arrived there, they realized that they had forgotten to bring any bread with them. And so, they were feeling a bit worried about what Jesus might say to them. When Jesus began to talk to them about the Temple establishment, warning them to beware of the "leaven" of the Pharisees and Sadducees, the disciples weren't sure what he meant. They mumbled to each other, "Jesus must mean we shouldn't buy bread from a baker who associates with the Pharisees or Sadducees. He must have said that because we showed up without any bread!" You see, the idea that being a devout Jew meant you were careful about whom you associated with was so ingrained in the disciples that they immediately jumped to this default.

But Jesus caught on to what they were muttering about, and he addressed them right away: "Do you really think that I care which baker you patronize? Don't you still understand the way I teach? Even after spending so much time as my disciples? So, you showed up without any bread. So what? Don't you remember that we fed five thousand people before with only five rounds of flatbread? Don't you remember the excess we had afterward? When I am talking about 'leaven,' I'm not talking about what we will eat for dinner! I will say it again: avoid the leaven of the Pharisees and Sadducees."

Finally, the disciples got it! Jesus didn't mean the bread you literally eat, but the "food that feeds your soul." He was speaking in metaphor. He was warning them against following the ways of the Pharisees and Sadducees.

So often in our reading of Scripture, in our understanding of Jesus, and even in our faith, we merely skim the surface of what Jesus meant for us to understand, or to be. So often we settle for easy literal answers and rules to follow, rather than seeking the depth and richness of what Jesus is really saying within our lives and challenging us with in our faith. Jesus is not in the business merely of feeding us a free lunch. Jesus is in the business of making us whole with him. Don't settle for a skim faith when you can have wholeness in mind, heart, and body with Jesus.

This lunch, have some "whole cheese" and pasta, a splurge today in your "fasting" to remind yourself of the wholeness and richness of the gospel and your in-depth relationship with the Lord. Cook pasta in boiling water. In a separate bowl, blend basil, parsley, pine nuts, and curd cheese, along with several tbsps of parmesan. Season with pepper. Add to the pasta and toss well. Garnish with basil and some extra parmesan.

Prayer

Lord, help me to understand the depth and breadth of your wisdom, the challenges of your words. Help me to immerse myself deeply in my relationship with you so that I understand not just with my mind, but through my faith. Amen.

SUPPER

You would think sometimes that the disciples just fell off the turnip truck when we see their interactions with Jesus. But then again, we all fall short of the saltshaker once in a while.

I was thinking about elementary school. Remember taking your boxed lunch each day to school? Those little metal latched cases with the pictures on the front? We all had them. All except for one boy in our grade. For the sake of anonymity, let's call him Daniel.

Daniel's mom worked. And in a rural place and time when most of the rest of our moms stayed home, this was an unusual thing to begin with. But then something new came to our town: McDonald's. I remember the fascination with this new and strange kind of take-out restaurant, a fascination and a suspicion about whether this constituted "real food." But at the same time, suddenly Daniel didn't come to school with a metal lunch box anymore. Instead, his mom would bring him a little brown bag each day from the magic "M" restaurant. And we all would be transfixed and terribly envious of the somehow elevated status of Daniel by this new food. We would have much rather seen Daniel carrying a lunch box like the rest of us. But soon some of the other boys began attempting to trade for (or at least to garner) some of those unusual looking "fries" and a sample of the slathered cheeseburger. They would take the treasured items and put them into their lunchboxes for safekeeping, so they could relish them at their tables and keep their prizes to themselves.

This is in a way how the disciples must have felt that day on the mountain when Jesus had his transfiguration experience before them! Suddenly, all Jesus' talk about being the Messiah took on a whole new meaning! And what is the first thing those disciples wanted to do? Put him in a box, of course! That way, they could treasure Jesus and the moment for safekeeping, and honor him among the other "treasured" prophets before him. But Jesus' identity was "out of the bag" at that point! And there was no going back.

When Jesus tabernacles with us, it's not about the lunch box anymore, but about a very different kind of food!

This evening, let Jesus feed your soul with something filling and new. I guarantee Jesus is not your ordinary supper but a living feast that will transform your heart and soul into a banquet of grace.

When you sit at your table with Jesus tonight, reminisce with him about the times he has surprised you with his presence in your life. Tonight, your supper with Jesus is a lentil and tuna salad. Mix together some tomatoes, lentils, and red onion. Make a dressing of oil, lemon juice, mustard, cumin, and coriander. Flake in the tuna, season with pepper, and enjoy this fresh, cold dish tonight.

Prayer

Lord, I need you to challenge me in my life to see differently, to hear with new ears, to be open to miracles, to make my life a witness to your amazing power. Amen.

24 Days to Resurrection

BREAKFAST: "COME AND 'BREAK THE FAST' WITH ME."

Jesus' breakfast on the beach is, in a sense, a fish tale, a reminder and a call to fish, feast, and feed. The risen Jesus calls his disciples from the fishing boat, where they are laboring intently, by telling them where to cast their nets. Then after bringing in nets full of fish, they come ashore to be welcomed by breakfast on the fire. Jesus tells them to bring some of their fish along too and add them to the meal. Then after they've feasted together, Jesus tells Simon, "If you love me, feed my sheep." Jesus needed to remind him of their mission and that he had the means to carry it out.

Sometimes we can get all fired up on Sunday for Christ, but when Monday comes, we return to our ordinary tasks, our jobs, and our own busyness, and we can forget our mission in life, the real mission that calls for us to "fish and feed." Not to mention the reminder that before we start our mission, we should always "feast" with Jesus. Always keep Jesus at your table. Jesus is at your table this morning calling you back from your work, your job, the places you are heading off to, the tasks in the kitchen, and the lists forming in your mind of things to do in the realm of ordinary living. He is calling you to the table with him.

"Come to breakfast," he says. "Come and break your fast with me. Feast with me. Come into this relationship with me this morning and let me remind you about what's important. You know," he says, "you have all of these skills you use in your work, but all these things you do are useless if you do them without keeping your eyes on the mission of the Kingdom. Don't worry so much about how to catch your fish. The fish will come. I'll show you how. Focus your attention on using what you have, what you can do, your skills and your means, to nourish others in the Way, the Truth, and the Life of God. If you keep your eyes on me, I will help you do all of it and more. Feed my people. Bring them to the table to dine with me."

This morning, start your day with cream cheese and lox (smoked salmon). Add some capers and put them onto a poppy bagel. Add a side of coffee and feast with Jesus as you prepare for your day.

Prayer

Lord, make my life a mission in your name. May my every task today be a reminder that without you in it, all of it is meaningless. Help me to be not just a "doer" but a "feeder," one who connects others to you. Amen.

LUNCH: INDIGESTION

"Get behind me!"

Peter had an especially hard time digesting Jesus' mission. He kept insisting that Jesus should not have to die and surely wouldn't.

He just couldn't accept the kind of messiah that Jesus really was. He remained invested throughout Jesus' ministry in a messiah who would rise up in his lifetime to establish another Jewish nation, or at least to establish a new kind of Temple authority. The disciples wanted a religious political leader. But Jesus was a sacrificial redeemer. The "polis" of Jesus was the kingdom of heaven, which included all humanity and all creation, bound and based only in love. Jesus' mission was hard to digest for almost anyone in his time for all kind of reasons.

What is hard for you to digest about Jesus' ministry? About his life? About his messianic role in your life? Take this time in your lunch break to spend some time with Jesus, the extraordinary healer. Ask him to heal your doubt, your need to make things different. Put your hands into his and feel the security of his love, the intent of his mission. Feel the confidence of his faith, the surety of his identity. Relax your mind, your body, and your soul into him. Let go of the fears of following Jesus into these last weeks of your journey. When you feast with Jesus today, set your mind on him and get behind him in his mission of redemption and love. Don't think "ahead" to what you want him to be in your life. But "get behind" where he will lead you in his.

Today, share a tuna niçoise salad with your luncheon guest: lettuce topped with eggs, new potatoes, green beans, cherry tomatoes, cucumbers, olives, anchovies, and tuna steaks. Top with pepper, clove, Dijon mustard, lemon juice, basil, and some olive oil. Add a side of sparkling water.

Prayer

Lord, make me a witness to your life and love. Let me follow you into every new territory and with the faith to see only as far ahead as your footsteps. Give me the strength to get behind you and be in mission to an ever-blooming kingdom. Amen.

Supper: Chicken Little

"The sky is falling!" says Chicken Little.

When the disciples all heard that Jesus would be betrayed into the hands of officials and killed, they barely heard the words, "He will be resurrected, newly alive on the third day!" They heard only "betrayed" and "killed," and they were filled with grief!

Have you ever been in an argument with someone, and perhaps you were so sure of what you felt was right or what you wanted to say that you couldn't "hear" what the other person was saying to you, or you heard only in part? We often hear Jesus this way too. We as disciples are people who see and hear in part. Sometimes the part we hear causes us undue distress. This is where our faith comes in. As humans, we will always know only in part. Most of life, most of what happens in our world, all of what will happen in the next, all of it dwells in a cloud of mystery. When we embrace that mystery, we will learn to live in what the Celts used to call "thin places." A "thin place" is that space between coming and going, a place of unmasking, a place where we dwell in "transitional space." For many, it is that space that knows not but is content in being. It is a sacred space, a frozen moment of true faith. Thin places suspend time and space, as though freeze-framing a picture, so you can contemplate it from a distance.

Tonight, let your supper with the Lord be your own "thin place." Look at the sunset in the sky with its reddish hue. When it disappears behind the horizon, enter into that thin place that acknowledges the sun's disappearance into dusk and yet knows that in the morning dawn, the sun will again rise. That is the place where your faith resides. Now set your mind on Jesus. Know in your mind and heart that though weeping may last the night, joy will come in the morning. Know that the resurrection is real, that Jesus is there beside you. Know.

Tonight, set upon your table a dish of spicy tomato chicken. Mix tomato paste, honey, Worcestershire sauce, rosemary, hot sauce, and other spices as you wish in a bowl. Add to it bits of cooked chicken and broil. Serve on a bed of couscous. With it, serve some broccoli with bits of orange rind and gingerroot, cloves, and soy. Make a fragrant tea. Then enter into your thin place for your time of prayer.

Prayer

Lord, when my faith is challenged and it feels like the world is falling in, lift me into your arms with you. Increase my faith. Erase my doubt. Let me feel your hand on my shoulder. Let me weep into the palm of your hand. Amen.

24 Days to Resurrection

BREAKFAST

"I am the true vine. Those who abide in me and I in them bear much fruit, because apart from me you can do nothing."

"You will know them by their fruits."

"I am like an olive tree flourishing in the house of God," says the psalmist (Psalm 52:8). What a statement of praise by someone with roots deeply and long invested in the Lord!

The Mount of Olives was Jesus' favorite place to pray outside of the city of Jerusalem, where he spent his last evenings the week of his death. Gethsemane (*geth* and *shemen*) means "oil press." This area is thought to be the origin of the tree of life. In Jesus' parable regarding the vineyard of olives, the trees must be nourished, pruned, and diligently cared for in order for them to bear good fruit.

Can you feel Jesus urging and nourishing you, as he does for all humanity? Can you feel the presence of the gardener seeking to secure your roots and guide your branches? He is the one advocating for you, giving you time to dine and spend time with him. Take time with Jesus each day. Allow him to nourish and provoke you in your faith and in your life. Let this time with him bear fruit in your life that will carry you into the arms of eternity.

"And I will dwell in the house of the Lord forever."

Today, spend your breakfast time in the garden with Jesus. Set your table with him in a place that will remind you of your root-edness in him. Enjoy the fruit of your relationship with the Lord and celebrate with a classic Mediterranean breakfast. Take apricot halves and spread them today with Greek yogurt. Drizzle the yogurt with honey, sprinkle with chopped pistachio nuts, and serve a cup of warm whole oats or brown rice with milk, cinnamon, almonds, and raisins or dried figs. Or make a sandwich made of rosemary focaccia bread with a thin layer of soft goat cheese, fresh tomato slices, and basil leaves.

Prayer

Lord, let my heart be rooted in you, my faith spread like the branches of the olive tree. May my life bear fruit in your name. Amen.

LUNCH

"For everything God created is good, and nothing is to be re-jected if it is received with thanksgiving, because it is consecrated by the word of God and prayer" (1 Timothy 4:4).

Have you ever seen an artist's shop filled with special individual items? These are usually shops that don't carry the ordinary machine-made factory things, but special things of all shapes and sizes, with an unusual flair or character. Many of these are hand-made, some made personally and especially for cherished customers. The tag

on those very special pieces of art often reads, "Created For You By
_____," and the artist's name follows. If you are the recipient of one
of these gifts, you know that the gift feels imbued with the unique
signature of the person who made it for you. And you cherish it
not only for its artwork but for the relationship and intimacy shared
between giver and receiver. The gift becomes a kind of "sanctified"
item for you, one that receives an honored place in your home, your
life, or in your heart.

This is the way we might look at God's creation and the bountiful food that the Lord has placed before us each and every day. Each
mealtime is a gift, not only of substance, but of the heart. When you
partake of a meal, you honor the giver. Each one of us is also part of
God's signature creation. Each one of us has been specially created to
be different and unique.

"And God saw that it was good."

In a sense, each of us wears a kind of identity marker upon our
hearts that reminds us that everywhere we look in God's beautiful
creation, we see signs that say, "Created for you by God."

Our acknowledgment of God's creative activity within our world
and within our lives can become our prayer. Each prayer over our
meal is a consecration, an acknowledgment, of God's many great and
creative gifts to us: the trees of the field, fruits of the vine, meat of
the land, and fish of the sea. And as we partake in prayer with God,
we embody the knowledge that this gift was created especially for us.

Just as Christ blessed the loaves and fishes, our prayers of thanks
consecrate our mealtime to the Lord, who created all creation as
nourishment to us. Know today that your meal with Jesus was made
by the Lord's hands: "Created by God for you." Especially for you.
Know that as you sit and dine with Jesus this lunchtime that he
receives your appreciation and honor with great joy. Eat and drink,
for it is good.

Today, join Jesus in prayer with a Mediterranean omelet. Beat eggs until frothy. Stir in parsley, pepper, turmeric, and chili powder. Heat oil and add egg mixture to skillet. Then add some cooked chopped onion, fennel, diced potato, clove, stuffed green olives, feta cheese, and marjoram. Serve with a tomato salad and iced pomegranate tea. If you don't like eggs, you can mix a warm rice salad of white rice, lemon juice, fresh oregano, pepper, tomatoes, black olives, feta cheese cubes, capers, and cilantro, and serve with pita bread.

Prayer

Lord, may my prayers be like a fragrant aroma to you, a sacrament of my thanks for this daily bread. May my life be as that food: consecrated to you. Lord, let it be good. Amen.

SUPPER: EAT YOUR SPINACH!

Ever since Popeye came to the Thimble Theatre in 1929, parents have been encouraging children to eat their spinach, so that they would grow big and strong. And "big and strong" for Popeye meant not only in body but in character too!

In the Scriptures, we find that the Word of God, embodied and digested, will make us even stronger, more faithful, more peaceful, and more joyful.

"When your words came, I ate them; they were my joy and my heart's delight, for I bear your name, Lord God Almighty" (Jeremiah 15:16).

Food is an intimate experience, and the "bread of life" is even more intimate. The sweetness of the Lord's love for us, the yeast of the kingdom, the fruit of the Spirit, and the body of Christ all tell us what a beautiful experience it is to partake of the heavenly banquet.

When we are called by God—and each of us are, each in a different and unique way— we embody that call as a sweet sacrament, and we incarnate the Spirit of Christ within us. The food of the gospel becomes the fullness of our soul. From that point on, our words, our actions, our love, and our faith will pour forth like honey naturally and organically.

"How sweet are your words to my taste, sweeter than honey to my mouth!" (Psalm 119:103).

When a bride and bridegroom cut the wedding cake together, they are sharing in the food of that covenant. Likewise, when we feast at the table with Jesus, we share in a covenant too, to become one with the living Lamb. Consecrated to God's service, our words and lives become likewise food and nourishment for others. We become people not only of soul but of substance.

God's words are food to a hungry soul: wholesome, nourishing, filling, sweet, and strengthening. Have faith in Christ's ability this mealtime to be the nourishment you need. Feed upon and digest the Word tonight so that it becomes part of you, for unless your feast is mixed with faith, it will not adhere to your bones.

Tonight, prepare a spinach salad with sprouts, hard boiled eggs, and oranges with a dressing of olive oil and balsamic vinegar mixed with honey and chives. Serve with a meal of spinach pie: mix together spinach, olive oil, chopped onions, pepper, and feta cheese, and place mixture into triangles of instant crescent dough. Roll up and seal. Skewer with a fork and bake for 20 minutes at 350 degrees.

Prayer

Lord, feast with me. Let our meal together be a sweet reminder of your magnificent love and grace that changes my life so that I can be a nourishment to others. Amen.

24 Days to Resurrection

BREAKFAST

"Turn away from me; let me weep bitterly. Do not try to console me over the destruction of my people" (Isaiah 22:4).

"As he approached Jerusalem and saw the city, [Jesus] wept over it" (Luke 19:41).

Often, the world can seem like a cold and difficult place. Still more often, we can feel that our actions don't make a difference or that our mission doesn't matter. Most of the time, our disappointment and disillusionment come more from the expectations we put upon ourselves than true concern about others.

We can find no better place in the Scriptures to see Jesus' humanity than in his fervent desire to save his people. All people. But even Jesus knew he couldn't save them all. Still, it never stopped him from fulfilling his mission in order to save the ones he could.

As a disciple of the Lord, you too may sometimes feel you do very little within the world. But if you have touched even one life with the healing touch of the Savior, if you have allowed even one person to find peace and joy in the gospel, if you have given the gift of Christ's overwhelming grace to even one, you have done already so very much.

This morning, as you break your fast with your Lord and Savior, know that he is crying along with you for all those in the world whose lives remain broken, all those who find it difficult to see, all those who are not yet safe within his loving arms.

Celebrate life this morning. Take a walk with Jesus. Look around at your world, watch the news, and read the headlines. Pray. Weep. Then go out and save the ones you can.

Today, harness your energy with a bowl of fruit, yogurt with granola and honey, and a slice of whole seeded toast. Add some juice and coffee to send you on your way.

Prayer

Lord, make me a willing servant of your saving grace. Send me out into the world with the strength of your Spirit and the tenderness of your tears. Amen.

LUNCH: WRAPPING IT UP

After spending some contemplative and preparatory time hidden away in quiet with his disciples in the outskirts of Ephraim, today Jesus is on the move. He prepares to make his way back into Judea. He knows this involves significant risk, but he also knows it's what he needs to do. Jericho is about an hour or so (five miles) away. It's Jesus' first stop. From there, he will make his way back toward Bethany.

After his perfumed anointing in Bethany, he will ride the palm strewn way into Jerusalem for the Feast of Unleavened Bread.

As Jesus wraps up his ministry on the road, you can feel his growing stress exuding from his body like the scent of that oiled perfume. He knows what is coming, and he doesn't want to be alone.

He asks you, "Will you join me as I walk this road? Can you? Will you?" You take his hand and walk his rock strewn path.

For lunch on the move, create today a wrap filled with your favorite foods—lettuce, tomatoes, egg salad or tuna, perhaps some ham and cheese, herbs, and mayo, and take it with you on your walk. Pair it with some vegetable juice and water in a handy thermos.

Now get in step with Jesus. The journey has only just begun.

Prayer

Lord, give me the courage to walk with you through places dark and unknown. Give me the faith of Bartimaeus, the zeal of Zacchaeus, and the passion to be in mission with you. Amen.

SUPPER: THE POWER OF FAITH

"And by faith the walls came down."

We all know the story of Joshua and the fall of Jericho's walls: the inhibiting separator between humankind and the Lord's Promised Land. What walls do you keep between Jesus and you?

The power of faith is highlighted in Jesus' final visit to the city of Jericho as he reenters the province of Judea. His visit is permeated by collapsing walls of doubt and separation in those whom he encounters.

Concealment can keep us from allowing Jesus to heal us the way we need to be healed in order to be made whole in God. All of us have walls we build around our hearts, around our spirits, within our minds, and within our lives. Some walls may come from negative past experiences. Some may come from difficulties in our interactions with others. Some may come from resistance to intimacy. All are rooted in some way in fear: fear of intimacy, fear of letting go of control, fear of authenticity, fear of surrender, fear of being seen.

Yet Jesus the beautiful healer comes to us unconcealed. If we approach Jesus wanting to be healed, we can give Jesus license to break through, break down, and break away our walls. For we cannot "see" when we've got "logs" in our eyes.

This evening, can you put aside your fears and let Jesus remove the obstacles that are keeping you from surrendering in trust to the Lord?

Tonight, allow someone else to prepare dinner for you. Allow yourself to be blindfolded and ask that person to feed you your food. Then do the same for him or her. Feel the trust that you must make in giving up control. Now imagine it is Jesus feeding you: Jesus in the life of another. Allow yourself to lose your fear and embrace your relationship with the risen Christ. Now rise up and follow him to Bethany.

I leave this menu blank tonight and allow you to be surprised and filled by another.

Prayer

Lord, take away my fear. Knock down my walls. Lift me up. Make me whole. Amen.

24 Days to Resurrection

BREAKFAST: ON THE ROAD— INVESTING IN THE JOURNEY, INVESTING IN THE KINGDOM

As we enter into the last ten days of our fast with Christ, we see Jesuspreparing his disciples for what is to come. Meanwhile, they are still vying for status within Jesus' "new kingdom," the one they imagine he's about to install. The disciples imagine a crown and a rule of law. Jesus imagines an alternative, invested community. And the time has come. He must teach them how to invest.

Speaking in parables, Jesus talks to his disciples about the value of investing in a special kind of Kingdom. The investments must be made by each and every person. The results will pay off over time. Mutual and large-scale "buy in" will ensure that the Kingdom will increase both in size and volume. Investment and encouragement will be part of the job the disciples have been trained to do.

Jesus explains that he must go on a long-term journey —one to a "distant country." If his disciples invest well, his kingdom will be thriving upon his return.

While everyone else waits for Jesus to effect change, Jesus lets people know that *they* are the change.

Many know the quote from Mahatma Gandhi, who once said in his lifetime in response to people waiting for the world to change, "Be the change you want to see in the world." Jesus says this first here, as recorded in the Gospel of Luke with the parable of the talents.

As you continue on your journey with Jesus today, begin to be the kind of Kingdom you want to see. Invest in your world with love. Be the voice of Christ in a world that needs change. Sow the seeds of the gospel into the lives of others. Show love to someone new each day. Make your life a journey of seed sowing, planting, and investing in the life of Jesus.

Fruit parcels are a way to take delicious warm fruit on the road. Place sliced apples, bananas, oranges, and other fruits into a large square of oil. Add a little butter, sugar, orange juice, and slivered almonds. Seal the packet and bake it on a baking sheet for 10 minutes. Open the packets for a warm fruit treat. Or pour it over some grape nuts with a side thermos of hot coffee.

Prayer

Lord, make me a granter of your peace. Help me to invest in you deeply, to invest deeply in loving others, to invest in deep roots, so that the olive trees of your kingdom may bear everlasting fruit. Amen.

LUNCH: JESUS RULES!

In Jesus' day, servants made a kingdom or an estate flourish. Those servants' investments in that kingdom were made possible through an original gift—a gift of means made by the master, the king. If you were loyal and served well, you could do well. Are you made by the Master? Is your life a gift to others? A gift you will invest? Are you a servant of the King? Jesus tells us the least will be first, and if you want to be first, you must be a servant to all. So, how low can you go?

As Jesus was making his way across the steep hills toward Bethphage and Bethany, Jewish people from all around were making their way to Jerusalem preparing for the Passover. Gossip raged as they looked for him everywhere they went, hoping to see him somewhere in the city. "Do you think he will decide not to come?" they asked. Meanwhile, the Pharisees ordered that if anyone knew where Jesus was, they must report his location immediately. Jesus was a wanted man. And his disciples were looked upon as "made" men, those who would be loyal to him. Yet the Temple officials sought for one who would betray that trust.

Have you been "made"?

The city of Jerusalem hummed like a beehive in the days before Jesus' arrival. It was only a day or two before the feast would begin, and each Jewish head of the family had begun the process of seeking a lamb. Soon each family would take a chosen lamb into the family home or place of residence for the duration of the week until the culmination of the festival, when the sacrifice would be made. The lamb needed to be unblemished. It would be kept as part of the family and loved as a pet in the days before the feast, when it would serve as a sacrifice for the ritual cleansing of sin for that family.

Today for lunch, prepare a special salad of greens with artichokes, olives, goat cheese, and oil. Accompany it with some Living Water. As you sit down today with Jesus, let him know you will be made new in him. That you choose him. That he is your Savior. As you prepare with him for the rituals leading up to the Passover, bring him into your home, hold him, love him. Tell him you will be his loyal servant.

Prayer

Lord, make me a servant of your kingdom. Give me the strength to serve well, the passion to serve with ardor, the love to serve with grace. Amen.

SUPPER

Six days before the Passover High Feast Day and two days before the Passover week-long celebration began, Jesus journeyed from Jericho (before going on to Jerusalem) to the village of Bethany (about two miles from Jerusalem), where Simon the Pharisee, a potter (note: the word used here most likely is *gariba* in Aramaic—Hebrew *grb*—which meant "potter," as opposed to *garoba*, which meant leper), hosted a large gathering of Jesus' friends, disciples, ministry patrons, and still-loyal Pharisees and colleagues at his home. Among those reclining around the table was Jesus' friend and benefactor Lazarus. Lazarus' sisters came too. Martha helped to serve, and true to form, Mary came in and welcomed the honored guest lavishly and extravagantly by anointing Jesus with an entire flask of expensive oil of spikenard—a combination of perfumed spices that filled the entire house with a sweet aroma that mixed with the sumptuous smells of the food.

This would be a final banquet shared by Jesus' supporters supporters—as well as those Pharisees within the Temple (most likely those left of the school of Hillel) who supported Jesus' ministry to the gentiles and felt him to be the awaited Messiah. What this Messiah was to be and do, however, was still a matter of disagreement among many, even many of Jesus' closest disciples. The events of this supper would mean a final turning point for Jesus and the broken straw for many, as they realized the extent of Jesus' aberration of what they thought the Messiah would be, or what they felt his entire ministry was about. Did he really think it was kosher to be welcomed and lavished with a $20,000 jar of expensive anointing oil, when that year's worth of money could have gone to the poor? Or to fund the future ministry of the group? How could he allow this woman to do this? Why didn't he chastise her and tell her to sell it and contribute it to the ministry fund instead? After all, they were all funding his ministry. How could he sanction such an extravagant act? How could he think such wastefulness of resources could be okay? Was he losing sight of what his ministry needed to be about?

Many felt they had misunderstood him. Some felt betrayed by him. Others were confused. Others were simply afraid, for they saw he was preparing for his death and that he really meant to allow it to happen. One in particular, Judas, would be determined to halt Jesus' reckless abandonment of Jewish values and bring this notorious, extravagant, and outlandish ministry to a final end. Especially when it threatened the making of money under the table, as Judas had a habit of helping himself to portions of the mission's purse. Jesus would again threaten the Temple purse strings a few days later when he would address the "under the table" undertakings of the Temple vendors and money changers set up for the Passover Feast that week.

While Judas may have thought Jesus would simply be stopped and prevented from what he considered to be going off the deep end, stopped from turning the tables on the money laundering industry, little did he know that once he sold Jesus into the hands of the authorities searching for him, he also sold his own soul. No one understood truly who Jesus was until after the resurrection, nor did they understand the true nature of his mission. But with the sweet smell of perfume still no doubt on his person, Jesus would be finally accused and convicted of apostasy, for which the punishment was (and still is in some Arab countries) immediate death.

This evening, imagine you are attending this very important social gathering, a banquet among Jesus' most ardent funders. Jesus is beginning to act strangely. To some, it feels as if he is abandoning his mission to revolutionize the Jewish nation, to establish the new kingdom. He has been saying odd things for weeks, telling them he will need to die. And none of them can understand why he would be giving up now. Most hope that once he gets to Jerusalem, things will fall into place. But tonight, he seems to have gone off the deep end. He allows a woman to anoint him with a $20,000 bottle of oil, saying she is the only one who understands him, saying she is preparing him for his mission to die. Many around the table are disturbed, to say the least. They whisper about what to do. You see Judas out of the corner of your eye. His eyes glint with anger. He feels betrayed by this man who has the power to change everything, the power to make him and these others the new leaders of the Temple, of a new kingdom.

Who are you at the table? What are you thinking? What will you do? Are you, too, losing hope that this rabbi will change the status quo? Change the world? Re-establish a new order? Take over the Temple? Do you know who he is? Will you join Mary? Will you follow him when he leaves for Jerusalem?

Tonight, celebrate with a banquet meal of Greek Pasticcio along with green beans and tomatoes and a Greek salad. Cook onion in water until it withers. Add ground meat seasoned with pepper, salt, and cinnamon. Add some tomato puree and butter and cook. Stir in a half cup of seasoned breadcrumbs and set them aside. Prepare a white sauce by heating butter. Add flour, salt, and pepper. Then add milk with egg yolk. Simmer and set aside. Prepare cooked macaroni. When done, mix into it the melted butter and grated cheese.

In a large oven pan, sprinkle the bottom with seasoned crumbs, then pour in macaroni and spread evenly on the base of the pan. On top of the macaroni, layer the ground meat, and then more macaroni. Pour white sauce over it, and top with remaining cheese. Bake one hour. Cook the green beans with seasoned tomato sauce and marjoram. Add a glass of red wine and lots of Living Water.

Prayer

Lord, in this turning point of my journey with you, keep me strong. Lord, make me a loyal disciple, a trusting follower, and an extravagant worshiper. Keep my eyes on you. Amen.

24 Days to Resurrection

BREAKFAST: THE "ISLAND" OF THE DAY BEFORE

"Does a clay pot dare argue with its maker, a pot that is like all the others? Does the clay ask the potter what he is doing? Does the pot complain that its maker has no skill? Do we dare say to our parents, 'Why did you make me like this?' The LORD, the holy God of Israel, the one who shapes the future, says: 'You have no right to question me about my children or to tell me what I ought to do!'" (Isaiah 45:9–11 GNT).

The morning after Jesus' anointing, Jesus found himself perhaps contemplating the events of the evening before and the reactions of his disciples, while now preparing and bracing himself for the upcoming week. Perhaps he spent some time remembering the faces of people he healed, the expectations of his people, the smiles of children, the love of this place. No doubt, too, he felt the lonely road he was coming to, as those around him refused to accept his mission to die. He knew they still hoped he would be the king they longed for, and they were waiting to cheer him on. He would encourage that hope, even as he knew the mission he would live out as Messiah would take them a while to understand. The people were all for a confrontation, which he had every intent of giving them. But he knew they didn't want to accept that their coming king would die. Nor did they understand the enormity of the coming resurrection. For them, it would feel like the end of their dream. But Jesus knew it was the restoration of God's dream, a bigger dream than any of them could imagine.

Jesus would spend this last day with his friend Lazarus, at his home, preparing to set off the next day to ride into Jerusalem on the Sabbath day, the day of the grand procession of the Paschal Lamb (the Lamb for the feast of Pesach).

This evening, Jesus (called by the Jews *Yahshua HaHotzri*, Prince of David, defender of the Halakha of Rabbi Hillel the Great) would meet with his disciples (*talmidim*) to go over the events of the coming week. The next day (the Saturday Sabbath, the tenth day of Nisan), Jesus would instruct his disciples to find a donkey and a colt tied to a neighbor's gate. Jesus knew the high priest would go through the Northern Damascus Gate and into the fields of Bethlehem on the day of the Sabbath to choose the unblemished Korban Lamb for the Pesach Temple Ritual. All the Jews would line the streets leading to the North Gate with fronds of palms and cedars to welcome the coming of the Paschal Lamb and the return of the high priest to the Temple to signal the start of the festival.

This morning, feel yourself in that place of waiting too. Spend some time in prayer with Jesus, looking back over the events of your life, the people you have loved, the events that have brought you joy. Pray along with the Lord for the strength of your mission too, the mission to step forward with Jesus into the world and to proclaim him Lord, even when others find it hard to see.

Make this a day of fresh bread, for a new day is coming. Share this meal with Christ, your Lord, and your Savior. He will lead you soon into life with him.

This morning, remind yourself of your humility before God. Bake some fresh artisan bread in a clay pot. Add yeast to 3 cups of warm water. Add 6 cups of flour, salt, rosemary, a dab of olive oil, and a hint of pepper. Mix well and let it rise for two hours. Dust with flour, slit, and bake at 450 for 35 minutes. Eat warm with an olive pate and fresh fruit. Complement with thick Greek hot coffee.

Prayer

Lord, let me this day and each day of my life remember that my life is in you, my joy found in you, my past rooted in you, my future assured in you. Amen.

LUNCH: "REDEEM WITH A LAMB EVERY FIRSTBORN DONKEY. ... REDEEM EVERY FIRSTBORN AMONG YOUR SONS" (EXODUS 13:13).

Rejoice greatly, daughter of Zion! Shout, daughter of Jerusalem! Look! Your king is coming to you: he is legitimate and victorious, humble and riding on a donkey—on a young donkey, the foal of a female donkey. (Zechariah 9:9).

"Say to Daughter Zion, 'See, your king comes to you, gentle and riding on a donkey, and on a colt, the foal of a donkey'" (Matthew 21:5).

Today Jesus calls together his loyal disciples to prepare them for his ride into Jerusalem on the Sabbath day. He tells them he will need them to untie a donkey and colt, to borrow them for his use. Jesus will take the place tomorrow of the Paschal Lamb, the lamb led to slaughter. He will be received as a redeemer, a king. The sacrifice he will make has not yet fully dawned upon the people.

As you sit at your table today with Jesus, how will you prepare yourself for the days to come? Let Jesus nourish you in spirit and in truth. Allow him to guide you in what you need to do in your life, as a disciple and as a lover of God, compassionate for his people. He is preparing you to "feed his lambs." Listen to him. Today, as you pray, take time for silence, for listening. Let Jesus' voice fill you, provoke you, exhilarate you, show you the way of the gospel. Prepare to walk in the Way.

Today is a day of preparation. Begin today to prepare your lamb roast with a citrus-herbal marinade. Mix together oregano, rosemary, thyme, the juice and zest of 1 lemon, olive oil, mustard, paprika, salt, and pepper, and rub the mixture over a lamb roast. Let it marinade in the refrigerator overnight or for up to two days. After you are through, put together a lunch of fresh roasted vegetables and hummus and savor your lunch slowly, as you pray about the days ahead.

Prayer

Lord, prepare me as your servant, the nourisher of your people. Guide me in ministry and in mission. Give me strength to love God with all of my heart, mind, soul, and strength. Amen.

SUPPER

Judas was missing for supper that night. As Jesus gathered with his inner circle to tell them what he wanted to do the next day for their ride into Jerusalem, Judas was nowhere among them. Jesus knew why. Later in the night, he would see the disciple slip in quietly. He said nothing.

Jesus and his disciples retired early, and Jesus went out, as he often did, to the Mount of Olives to pray. He needed to be alone for a while. More and more, people began gathering outside of Lazarus' home, waiting for Jesus to come out. They heard he was there and wanted to see him. Tomorrow, many of them would follow him all the way into Jerusalem.

Tonight, you and he are alone at the table. He has come back from the garden, and the hosts have gone to bed. Jesus is reclining near you, and in the candlelight, his face looks sad but strong and sure. When you look at him, he smiles. Take his hand now. Feel his quiet strength, his confidence, his love. He knows you will accompany him tomorrow as he begins on his way. And he welcomes you beside him. Tonight, you and he share a quiet moment. The last one, perhaps, for a while.

Dinner tonight is an array of finger foods: olives stuffed with feta cheese, grape leaves stuffed with rice and cheese, spinach pockets, bowls of artichokes, hearts of palm, nuts, and fava beans. A couscous with nuts and fruit can be scooped up with bits of matza. Another bowl contains berries and other Mediterranean fruits. Smoked fish and dipping oils with marjoram and basil surround the larger ones, flanked by fresh pita. A sparkling water mixed with berries, lime, and lemon quenches your thirst. Honey cakes with thick, hot coffee finishes up your meal.

You are quiet. You pray with him; thank him for the ordeal he will go through for you. For you and all of the others. Together, you read together from Psalm 118 (paraphrased here): "God is with me, so I will not be afraid of anything. ... He is my strength, and he is the reason I sing. ... He who comes in the name of the Lord will be blessed. ... Let the feast begin. ... You are my God, and I praise you.

Give thanks to our Eternal God; He is always good. He never ceases to be loving and kind."

Tonight is a night to be thankful. A night to prepare. A night of quiet realization for what God will do for you. He has come to save you. Yes, even you. He has come for you.

Prayer

Lord, I am overwhelmed this day by the depth and breadth of your love, the immensity of your willing sacrifice. Make me willing to walk with you. Keep me from fleeing. Lead me onward. Take me home. Amen.

24 Days to Resurrection

BREAKFAST

"God is with me, ... so when I look at those who hate me, victory will be in sight. It is better to put your faith in God than to trust in people. It is better to put your faith in God than to trust in rulers. ... God has been there to save me in every situation. ... I will not die. I will live. I will live to tell about all that God has done. Open wide to me the gates so that I may walk through them and offer praise and worship to the Lord our God. ... The stone that the builders rejected has become the very stone that holds together the entire foundation. This is the work of God, and it is marvelous in our eyes. This is the day that God has made; let us rejoice and be happy in it. Let the feast begin. Bring the sacrifice and tie it to the horns of the altar." (Paraphrase of Psalm 118—for the Procession of the Lamb, beginning the Feast of Unleavened Bread)

This is the day of choosing the Korban Pesach (the unblemished lamb chosen by the High Priest Caiaphas from the fields of Bethlehem). Caiaphas will choose the lamb and will bring it into Jerusalem via the Procession of the Lamb through the Northern Damascus

Gate. And all families will take their lambs into their households to love them until the time of sacrifice at three p.m. on the fourteenth day of Nisan (Wednesday).

Jesus is awake early and preparing a breakfast of unleavened bread (matzo), goat cheese, and fruit. You help by making thick coffee on the stove and adding some cooked oats with honey and nuts.

As you sit around the table with Jesus, he tells you that today the unblemished lamb will be chosen and brought to the Temple in the procession. This afternoon, the high priest will choose a lamb from the Temple fields in Bethlehem, then he will enter the gates of Jerusalem with the lamb, the Korban Pesach, and bind it to the altar. And this will mark the beginning of the salvation of God's people, the final Passover, as foretold in the Exodus story (chapter 12).

Then Jesus looks directly at you. And he asks you if you know who he is.

You answer, "Jesus, you are the Lamb of God, the chosen one, the one who will sacrifice and save God's people to atone for us and to make us one again with God, to return us to our original covenant, to make us wholly human, as we were intended to be. You are the lamb, the Korban Pesach."

Jesus nods. He says, "Let the time of fasting begin, the time to unloose the ties of sin that bind God's people and keep them from becoming free in him. It is time to prepare for the Passover Feast that will be the Garden Banquet of Glory, the return of all creation to God in overflowing mercy, bountiful love and wholeness, and salvation for all God's people. The sacrifice of the Lamb will make it so."

He looks around at all of his disciples at the table. He says, "Today, it begins." Together, you sing Psalm 118.

Jesus tells you that after breakfast, you will accompany the others to the neighboring town of Bethphage, where you will find a donkey and colt tied there. He instructs you to untie it. As you do, the words of the book of Exodus and the prophet Isaiah from your morning prayers with Jesus come into your mind:

"Redeem with a lamb every firstborn donkey. … Redeem every firstborn among your sons" (Exodus 13:13).

"Is not this the kind of fasting I have chosen: to loose the chains of injustice and untie the cords of the yoke, to set the oppressed free and break every yoke?" (Isaiah 58:6).

You bring the donkey and its colt to Jesus, who is preparing to make his way now from Bethany to the Mount of Olives. A crowd is already gathering.

Prayer

Lord, may this day mark a "fast" time in my life, a day in which I will let go of the past and embrace a future with you. Help me to unloose the doubts that bind me. Help me to stay rooted and confident in you. Amen.

LUNCH

Today, you will help Martha prepare a shepherd's pie for the evening meal before you get on your way to Jerusalem. Jesus and his disciples will be hungry after the ride into the city, and you want to be prepared. And then you join the others at the table, where a brief lunch is waiting.

Upon returning from Bethphage with the donkey and colt, the disciples prepared the animals for the trip, gathered blankets to use for saddles, and had them fed and watered. Then they came in to pray a while with Jesus. Now, at the luncheon table, Jesus again goes over the way the day will go.

Lunch today consists of fresh bread topped with some smoked fish, cheeses, and dried tomatoes, which are then toasted on the fire. A thick coconut milk with rice topped with cardamom makes a pudding to accompany it.

There is little time until the journey begins now. At the close of the meal, all of you gather outside. As all of you begin the trip back toward the Mount of Olives, more and more people gather around the donkey and her colt, being led toward the western gate of Jerusalem. You can hear the sounds of the crowd already gathered in Jerusalem at the Northern Gate. They've gathered bunches of palm fronds, along with branches of other native trees. There, lining the streets of Jerusalem from gate to Temple, they wait, as Caiaphas goes out to choose the lamb for the High Feast. You can almost see him in the fields, talking to the shepherds, assuring that the lamb he chooses will have no blemish. These are the shepherds descended from David, those watching over the Temple flocks, the largest and best in the region. From their towers, they can see all the way to the Temple itself. They are honored to take part in this holy day. As they prepare the lamb for the processional of the high priest, they sing the psalms. Back in Jerusalem, the crowd is singing too, Psalm 118, to welcome the Paschal Lamb to the Temple for the annual Sabbath of Passover, to take place on Thursday. Today, Saturday, is the weekly Sabbath, and after the procession, all families will take their own chosen sheep into their homes to await the day of sacrifice on Wednesday. On Wednesday afternoon at three o'clock, the lamb will be slain and the meat prepared for the High Feast to take place on Thursday.

You can hear them singing as Jesus and his entourage come around to the western wall of the city. It is about to begin.

Prayer

Lord, give me strength to endure what is to come, in my life and in my faith. Challenge me to walk with you, to follow you into difficult places, to live out the gospel in the world, even in a world that does not understand its own gift. Amen.

SUPPER

Jesus waited at the western gate with his disciples, and a donkey with her two-year-old colt. He looks around at all of his disciples and nods. It is time. The disciples throw their cloaks upon the animals for Jesus to sit on. Then they go ahead to open the Northern Gate of Damascus that will allow Jesus to enter in. They motion for you and the others to follow, leaving Jesus behind, so they can prepare his entry. Some of the crowd remains, throwing their cloaks in the donkey's path as Jesus begins to ride. Jesus mounts, then descends from the Mount of Olives into the Kidron Valley toward Jerusalem.

He sent the disciples on ahead to announce his arrival as the fulfillment of what the prophet Zechariah had foretold in Zechariah 9:9. Following the disciples' path, Jesus circles around to the north and heads toward the Northern Damascus Gate. Meanwhile Caiaphas is still in the fields choosing the Paschal Lamb. The people are gathered by the thousands, and many are already chanting the words of Psalm 118, "Hosanna in the highest! Blessed is he who comes in the name of the Lord!"

Suddenly, the disciples arrive and yell out the prophetic words. The gate opens for the return of the high priest with the Paschal Lamb. But it is not Caiaphas with the lamb, but Yeshua (Jesus, the Lamb of God), who comes riding through the Damascus Gate, sitting on a young colt! He is riding a donkey—the symbol of the Jewish people in need of unburdening from captivity, in the procession meant for their Redeeming Lamb. Some begin to realize Jesus' intentions. With his symbolic ritual, Jesus has answered the people's yearning for a king and liberator, but not in the way they expect. He will let them know that his mission will be even greater—the fulfillment of the messianic prophesy and God's salvific act of atonement. Others miss the meaning of Jesus' coming. They are too caught up in their own vision.

As Caiaphas prepares to enter from the fields, the people's attention has already been diverted. As soon as they see Yehshua, their beloved healer and revolutionary, they begin shouting loudly and waving their palms. "He has decided to come to the festival after all!" "He has come to establish the new Kingdom!" The crowd becomes fervent, engaging in a fanfare to welcome the infamous rabbi. They wave their branches passionately. The disciples encourage them. Alarmed now (and with the priestly Passover procession disrupted), the Shammaites (the Pharisaic School in charge) begin rebuking Jesus, shouting for him to silence his disciples. Jesus shouts back, "If these were silenced, the very stones would cry out!"

As the crowd becomes ecstatic, they begin throwing off their cloaks and throwing them onto the ground in his path, welcoming the great Messiah to the Festival of Unleavened Bread—the celebration of the great Exodus! To the Temple, Jesus rides to say the prayer, the reading from Exodus 6: "I will bring you out … deliver you … redeem you … take you for my people … and I will be your God … gather all peoples … bring you into the land I have promised to be with me." And as he approaches the great Temple in Jerusalem, tears stream down his cheeks, and he says in anguish, "Jerusalem, Jerusalem, how I wish you knew today what would bring peace! But you can't see. You don't recognize the day when God's Anointed One is with you."

At this, Jesus strides quickly into the Temple and begins driving out the Temple merchants, who have set up their tables and are doing business right in the midst of the prayer space, keeping the people who want to pray and worship from doing so. The vendors make huge amounts during festival days and are intent on maximizing the revenue for the Temple (and what they can get for themselves on the side), buying and selling wares, selling sacrifices for exorbitant prices, and changing money to collect Temple taxes right in the Temple prayer courts. Jesus drives them all out of the Temple and into the courtyards, releasing all of the animals set for slaughter. He turns over their benches and upsets their tables, saying, "The Hebrew Scriptures tell you, 'My house shall be a house of prayer for all people,' but you have turned it into a thievery!"

After Jesus restores the prayer space to the people, they rush in to see him, all those who have been shut out by the authorities: the lame, the children, and many others. And Jesus spends time healing and teaching as the children sing: "Hosanna to the Son of David!" The priests and scribes rush in, confused by the overturned tables, those who were healed praising God, and the children singing. They are shocked and angry. They say to him, "Are you going to allow these people and children to do this? To say these words?" Jesus stands up: "Yes! Haven't you read your own psalter? From the mouths and souls of infants and toddlers, the most innocent! You must immerse yourself in repentance!"

Jesus leaves Jerusalem a while later to travel back to Bethany once again, where he spends the night. Meanwhile, the Temple is buzzing with anger and indignation. They are angrier than they've ever been. Jesus is threatening everything they stand for. They know something has to be done.

When Jesus arrives back in Bethany, exhausted and spent, you welcome him with the shepherd's pie, a dish of mashed potato mixed with parsley, onions, matzo crumbs, and pepper over your ground lamb meat with tomato sauce, butter, rosemary, thyme, cinnamon, oregano, and matzo crumbs. You have mixed into it some cooked carrots, corn, and peas, and you have baked it at 400 degrees for one hour. A side of olives and goat cheese accompanies your Living Water.

Tomorrow, Jesus will return to the Temple. Spend this night with him in prayer, quietly. See the strength and determination in his dark eyes, the love in his tears. Comfort him. He is your Savior.

Prayer

Lord, prepare me for the events of this day, and every day spent with you. Help me to see what is most important in my life and to keep my heart grounded in your mercy and your love. Amen.

24 Days to Resurrection

BREAKFAST: A TIME OF WAITING ...

"Now you dwellers in Jerusalem and people of Judah, judge between me and my vineyard. What more could have been done for my vineyard than I have done for it?" (Isaiah 5:3–4).

God came to his people. And yet they did not recognize him.

Jesus rose early today. He slept fitfully in the night, knowing that the time had come, and he could not go back from here. The events that would lead to his death had been set in motion. Now would be a time of waiting for his divine mission to unfold. God's time of dwelling among humankind would soon end, and it would be long before God would again walk among creation. But Jesus would affect a divine act that would redeem anyone who would come to him, so that they could be made whole. And then he would return in final triumph to establish his garden kingdom.

"'In that day each of you will invite your neighbor to sit under your vine and fig tree,' declares the LORD Almighty" (Zechariah 3:10).

For now, the tree lay barren and withered, but it would bloom again. You cannot harvest from a vine with withered roots. They would need to be re-established. His disciples would do that in his absence. As from the beginning of time, God would begin again with the people. And again. And again.

"And now Jerusalem," Jesus says, "as for the Temple you have hewn to keep out my precious little ones, 'I will break down its wall, and it will be trampled' (Isaiah 5:5). But the time will come again when I will build it up into a spiritual house, a house with many rooms, a tree where all may dwell in its branches." Psalm 118:22 echoes in his mind: "The stone the builders rejected has become the cornerstone." He says, "The living stones of my disciples will raise up a spiritual temple upon my foundations, and all people will dwell in the house of the Lord always. The rock will be rolled away, and the fruit of the Tree of Life given to you."

Jesus leaves early and fasts until he comes again into the Temple to teach and heal among the people who crowd in to see him, so you will fast too. He will have no fruit to show for his journey from the fig tree of Jerusalem. But he knows new trees will be planted by the little ones he now lets in.

Prayer

Lord, as I fast this morning, let me listen to your voice, hear the proclamation of your salvation, feel in my very bones the change that is coming in my heart and in my world. Amen.

LUNCH: THE TRAPPINGS OF THE TEMPLE

When Jesus got to the Temple, he began to teach, and he taught there the entire day long. He taught in parable after parable. In the manner that Nathan confronted David, Jesus tried to confront the chief priests and elders (Pharisees) with those parables. Again and again, he confronted them with the psalm they had themselves sung for the festive procession: Psalm 118. "The rock rejected has become the cornerstone." Again and again, he confronted them with their own hypocrisy. But he knew he could not get through to them. Each time he came close, the very foundations of his arguments blindsided the Temple officials, and they trampled on his words in anger.

They had a mind only to entrap him. Meanwhile, Jesus continued to present parables to the crowds, who sat in the Temple to hear him clearly speaking against the trappings of the Temple under the rule of the current Sanhedrin. He came back every day to teach in the Temple, as the chief priests and religious scholars tried to think of a way to have him killed. He was enormously popular, and they were afraid to do anything too hasty.

The Pharisees schemed. Of course, the people loved Jesus because he told them they would be first in the kingdom of God, ahead of all of the officials. This angered the Temple priests and elders. Jesus was making a fool of them in front of the people. Their authority was being be undermined.

Jesus tricked them again and again. Today, he had told them a story of a father who asked two sons to work in his vineyard. Since the Pharisees identified only themselves as "sons" of the Father, they didn't immediately see where Jesus was going. The first declined to go, but later he changed his mind and went to work. The second son said he would go but never did. Jesus asked the priests and scholars, "Which son did as the father asked?" They all answered, "The first." But Jesus then said, "Listen to me. These tax collectors and prostitutes are 'sons' of God too, and they are going to be the ones who enter the kingdom of God ahead of you! They heard John's call to repent, and they did! But you refuse to listen and change your ways!"

Knowing they had been tricked into revealing themselves, the scholars and priests steamed. They looked around at the people gathered there. Jesus had dared to embarrass them in front of everyone. Did he really want to tell these dirty children, gentile tax collectors, and even women that they were "children" of God? They were people who were not clean and shouldn't even be in the Temple. He had let all of them in. And now he was degrading the scholars and priests in front of them. He needed to be stopped. They needed to figure out how to trip him up. Sooner or later, he would say the wrong thing ...

After a while, Jesus got up to take a break. The people would wait for him to return that afternoon.

Today, Jesus has a lot to do, and he will take only a brief time for lunch. You go with him as he climbs the hill to the Mount of Olives to have a short prayer and a lunch of fruits, bread, and cheeses. Take your lunch outdoors too. Sit with him as he prays.

Prayer

Lord, let me never be tired of hearing your stories. May I find myself within them and keep my heart resting not in the distractions of others, but only in You. Amen.

SUPPER: ON GOD'S VINEYARD

Today, prepare a supper of Moroccan chicken with lemon and olives and a side of couscous. Jesus will arrive back from the Temple at sundown, and all of you will gather around the table.

Season cut-up chicken with salt and pepper and brown it in olive oil until almost done through. Remove the chicken and sauté onions, carrots, and celery. When tender, stir in ginger, paprika, cumin, oregano, cayenne, and turmeric. Mix in chicken or vegetable broth and tomatoes. Sauté zucchini with lemon juice and add it and the chicken back into the pan and simmer. Serve with couscous and black olives, raisins, and cilantro.

As you prepare the evening meal, you think about the stories Jesus taught today at the Temple. He spoke of God's vineyard several times. You think about being God's tenant. About tending the sweet fruit of the vineyard well, keeping it healthy, fruit-bearing, prospering, growing, nourishing, and beautiful. You know that in order to serve the Owner, you must focus on tending and keeping the Garden of God, staying in relationship with the Lord, humbly living in God's creation, serving with love and nourishing others, staying loyal to the One who provides. Jesus accused the Temple priests and elders of instead wanting to usurp the ownership of God. Each time God would send a representative to collect fruit from them, the ungrateful tenants would attack those representative servants instead. And when God sent his Son, the tenants wanted to kill him and take over his place.

You think about Christ's temple, the spiritual temple of those faithful to God, who want to serve and be loyal to the Lord. And how easy it is, when you haven't seen the Master in a while, to imagine that the vineyard is your own to order as you wish.

As you hold a fistful of olives in your hand, you make a new resolve to spend more time in the vineyard, to get to know the others who have recognized Jesus as Lord. To focus more on the feast and preparing every meal according to God's recipes of love and nourishment for all people, to listen more to Jesus' way to tend the vineyard, and to spend less time trying to cook up a plan for a better way to do it.

Prayer

Lord, sometimes I tend to think I have you all to myself. But you share your meal with so many who need you. Let me be part of your household. Let me be a loyal servant who asks little and gives much. Amen.

24 Days to Resurrection

BREAKFAST

Have a bowl of oatmeal with fruits and nuts and a side of coffee with Jesus this morning. No time for much more. Jesus is off to the Temple again early to teach. And he will spend the day there once again sparring with the Temple scholars, pushing their buttons. He knew he would eventually goad them into a final confrontation that would seal his mission and change the course of history for God. You go along with him and the others. Yesterday, Jesus told the story of the wedding banquet. Much like with the story of the vineyard, Jesus continued to chastise the Temple authorities in their misunderstandings of God's kingdom. To let them know again that those they want to keep out will be first at the Lord's table. Each time he proclaimed himself as Messiah, the Son of God, and with stories, letting them know his authority came from God. Today, the Pharisees will send the Temple students to him to try to trip him up. The scholars and priests keep thinking of people to send to Jesus to vex him. They send spies who pretend to ask sincere questions, when really they are listening for anything he says that they can use to justify his arrest.

They know it is the only way they can take him down. For he is one of them, a powerful presence in the Temple and in the community.

Prayer

Lord, in the tumult of my life, when so many question your identity and your power in the world, let my heart be filled with the joy of you. Let my soul be humbled by your presence in my life. Amen.

LUNCH

The students came with the scholars and priests and elders, pretending to take the opportunity to hear the great rabbi speak. They said, "Teacher, we respect you because you speak and teach only what is right. You show no partiality to anyone, and you truly teach the way of God. So ... is it lawful for us to pay taxes to Caesar's occupying regime, or should we refuse?" The Pharisees thought that if they used the students, Jesus would be tricked into saying something that could convict him, but Jesus saw through it right away.

Jesus gave them an answer they couldn't get around: "Show me a coin. Whose image and name are on it?"

"Caesar's," they replied.

"Then you give to Caesar what belongs to him and give to God whatever is God's."

Of course, Jesus knew they would understand everything in the created world belongs to God. And yet he had not literally undone the secular law. He had challenged them with their own dilemma. He would refuse to be dragged into a political conversation. He would not allow them to make him into a superficial leader, a secular, political revolutionary, when he was so much more than that. With his answer, he solidified his identity once again as Son of God. The students tried again to question him on all manner of things, including the nature of the resurrection, but to no avail.

Finally, Jesus asks a question of them, and now he turns to you, his disciples, to make sure you see the difference between the Temple scholars with their pride and their motives, and those whose faith sustains them and who give to others from their humility. The Temple officials were more interested in sustaining the Temple—its rules, opulence, building, and their control—than in sustaining God's covenant for all people. Jesus turns to the visitors and tourists, and he says, "Go ahead, look around, and be impressed. But days are coming when one stone will not be left standing on another. Everything will be demolished." The crowd gasps. Jesus will spend that afternoon telling them about the days to come.

For lunch today, provide a plate of hummus with vegetables. Or roll it into a wrap with roasted veggies and sprouts, tomatoes, and olives. Eat it knowing it is food from God's great garden.

Prayer

Lord, let each morning be an epiphany of my faith. Help me understand you, not just with my head but with my heart. Let me see in my life what is truly important in the eyes of God. Amen.

SUPPER: TOURIST OR KINFOLK

"For we were all baptized by one Spirit so as to form one body—whether Jews or Gentiles, slave or free—and we were all given the one Spirit to drink" (1 Corinthians 12:13).

After lunch, you accompany Jesus again to the Temple. He will be there every day now until his arrest. On the way, you meet up with some Greeks pilgrimaging to the festival in Jerusalem. They are considered gentiles, and they've been hoping to meet Jesus, the friend of gentiles, the one who is different from the other rabbis and priests. An entire crowd of people, some foreigners, and some locals gather and follow Jesus every time he comes into the city to speak in the Temple. They want to hear what the great teacher has to say.

As you look around, you see some of them approach Philip, who is at the back of the group. They are Greeks. One of them asks Philip if they could please meet the rabbi. Andrew and Philip go on ahead to let Jesus know of their request.

Jesus turns and speaks to the group of people following him. He tells them he is the Son of God and lets them know that his mission is God's mission, that all of them will be drawn into God's kingdom when he is lifted up. He tells them the time has come and explains it with a parable: "Very truly I tell you, unless a kernel of wheat falls to the ground and dies, it remains only a single seed. But if it dies, it produces many seeds" (John 12:24). "Anyone," he says, "who wants to be with me will be so honored by God. Not just Jews. But any of you," he says. "when I am lifted up from the earth, I will draw all people to myself" (John 12:32). Many do not understand this parable, although they understand that a seed must "die" in order to grow into a living plant that will bear fruit and feed others. But Jesus is trying to prepare the people for his death and to let them know that out of his death, life will be born for every one of them, Jew or Greek, slave or free. There will be no designations in heaven. He told the Sadducees this earlier today—that there is no marriage in heaven, but in resurrection, all live a different kind of resurrected life. Now, he explains that there is no hierarchy, no preference, no status in God's holy covenant. All are welcomed into God's loving arms. And all those who want entry, who will follow him, God's Son, who want to change their lives to live out of love, will receive it because of him.

Jesus tells them, "The light of God is among you in me, the Messiah, Emmanuel. When you choose to walk with the light, to follow me, no darkness will ever surround you again. Even when the light goes out from the world, when your faith is firmly rooted in the light of my resurrection, you will be reborn as daughters and sons of the light. All of you are children of God through me."

Many of the people were fascinated by Jesus, but they didn't understand him. And they didn't know how to trust in what he was saying. But there were many, too, who put their faith and lives in him entirely in secret. They wouldn't declare it openly for fear of the Pharisees and their threats to expel all of Jesus' followers from the synagogue. But many followed Jesus in their hearts.

Jesus knew this and encouraged them, saying as he left the crowd, "Anyone who puts their faith in me also puts their faith in God. I have come to free the world from the shackles of blindness about God's love. Through me, all the world may be freed to see themselves as children of God. I haven't come to judge the world. That is left to the Father at the end of times. I have come as his incarnated Son to gather all of you in, to welcome you into the Father's arms. To let you know our God is your God. God's covenant is your covenant. And his kingdom belongs to all of you. My words are God's, and God's are mine."

Through this whole period of time, Jesus taught in the temple each day. People would arrive at the temple early in the morning to listen. Then, at day's end, he would leave the city and sleep on the Mount of Olives (Mount Olivet). This daily pattern continued as they came closer to the feast of Unleavened Bread, also known as the Passover.

After Jesus had spent the day teaching again in the Temple, he again climbed the road back to the Mount of Olives toward Bethany, to Lazarus' house, where he was staying.

As you gather for supper, Jesus talks to all of you, all of his disciples, about what you learned that day.

Your supper consists tonight of fish baked in the oven and topped with lemon and olives. A side of roasted eggplant and zucchini accompanies the meal. As you pass around the wine, all of you pray together.

Prayer

Lord, may my heart be open to all people. Help me to follow you even when the road gets hard and long. Help me to keep my eyes open in the world, to see every person as God's child, to encourage every person to get to know you, and to welcome every person as a treasure of God's kingdom. Amen.

24 Days to Resurrection

BREAKFAST

Jesus rises again early today. You meet him at the table and share together a bowl of creamed wheat with raisins and nuts. On the side are prunes, figs, dates, and other fresh fruits. You finish making the coffee and bring it to the table. Jesus tells you his time is getting short. Today, he will again teach in the Temple. It is now only a few more days until the Passover Feast, and he wants to prepare you for what is to come. You look at his determined face. And you say that you wish he wouldn't have to die. But he insists it is the only way. It is God's way. He tells you to remember the parable of the wheat. He cannot live to resurrect all those in the world until he first goes through this earthly death. But then, all power and authority will be his to bring all people back to God.

You try to understand. It's hard. But you will trust him. And you tell him so.

You finish your breakfast. And then you prepare to go back to the Temple with the others.

Prayer

Lord, give me the faith that moves mountains. Give me the faith in you that can transform my life from seed to flower. Give me the confidence to follow you all the way from cross to garden … all the way into God's arms. Amen.

LUNCH

Jesus looks troubled when he comes to the garden on the Mount of Olives. His eyes had a distant look of great sadness. You see him coming and lay down a cloth on the grass to sit with him for a while. You have brought pitas filled with fresh vegetables tossed with cilantro. On the side, you have brought some spicy tomato soup in a large bowl, enough for several to share, and lots of water. You sit and eat with him silently, waiting for him to speak to you.

He tells you that as he speaks, one of his disciples, Judas Iscariot, is meeting with the chief priests and religious scholars in the Temple. He set up a private meeting with them. The Temple police have been called in to listen. The Temple officials are delighted. This is the break they have been looking for. They agree to a hefty payment to Judas if he will betray his master teacher, Jesus. Judas tells them he will let them know the moment.

When Judas came in the night before, he didn't look at Jesus. He just went to his room. But Jesus knew.

Today, it is lunchtime, and Judas is missing. Jesus knows it will now be a matter of days. He has little time left. He takes your hand. His hand is warm and strong. Then he smiles at you, and he tells you that this is what needs to be done. It will be hard. But when it is finished, he will be with you again. And nothing will keep you from him, or from the Father, again.

It is soon time to return to the Temple. Jesus helps you to your feet, and hand in hand, you walk back down the mountain and through the gate to Jerusalem.

Prayer

Lord, my loyalty to you is unshakable. I will be with you to the end of time. And you will be my salvation. Help me to stay by your side through every calamity, to know you are the light and the way to God, and the life of wholeness and peace. Amen.

SUPPER: SIGNS

Through this whole period of time, Jesus teaches in the Temple each day. You watch the people crowding in to see him. People will arrive in the Temple early in the morning to listen. Then, at day's end, he will leave the city and sleep on the Mount of Olives. This continues each day as you come closer and closer to the Feast of Un-leavened Bread, also known as the Passover (Pesach).

This afternoon Jesus spends time telling the crowds of people who came to see him of the events that will soon come—events that will eventually destroy the Temple as they know it. Just as he told you at lunch, he warns them to stay alert but not to be afraid. He tells them that their freedom to openly worship God, their liberation from the rejections, restrictions, and ostracizing effects of the religious laws, will soon be here. They will be part of God's coming kingdom.

Then he speaks vehemently this afternoon to all who are gath-ered, and to the many who have come this day to see him. He speaks so powerfully and forcefully that by end of day, he is exhausted and spent. He will have only one more day to teach in the Temple. Each day, his messages become harsher and more pointed at the Temple Pharisees and priests, scholars, and elders.

He begins talking to his disciples and the others gathered here. He tells them though they should do the things the Pharisees and scribes instruct them to do, yet they should not imitate the way they act, for there is a big difference in what they say and the way they carry out their lives. They do not "walk the talk." Just the opposite! They are narcissistic and vain, and they love to flaunt their self-righteousness and power, love their leadership roles and their lofty titles. But, Jesus says, "If you are ever recognized for anything, let it be only for your service. For whoever humbles him or herself will be exalted by God, not the opposite."

Then he turns to the Pharisees and legalists: "There is such a gulf between what you say and what you do. You would stand before a crowd and lock the door of the kingdom of heaven right in front of everyone. But hear this—you won't enter it yourselves!" Jesus hurls admonishments at the Temple scholars and priests again and again. With pointed language and sharp criticism, he publicly chastises them for all of their hypocritical actions that go entirely against the covenant of God that they were appointed to represent. He calls them merciless and unfaithful, murdering snakes, with blood on their hands. And he accuses them of all of the murdering deeds that they have done and will continue to do in order to maintain their power. He tells them he longed to gather them into the kingdom of God, but that they refused to listen and be gathered. They have therefore chosen their heritage, and God will remove his blessing from them. Then he turns to the shocked crowd once again and quotes the psalmist: "Anyone who truly comes in the name of the Lord God will be blessed!"

The rooms are silent. Not a sound is heard. Jesus gets up then, and he leaves the Temple.

His disciples get up quickly and run after him. You get up with them. Out of the corner of your eye, you can see the angry and vengeful looks on the faces of the Temple officials. They are turning to each other, and you can see the glint of determination in their eyes. Their minds are made up. They will wait now to hear from Judas. Smugly, they sit back. They will have their say. And their unruly colleague will be finished.

A cold chill passes through you as you hear their angry words. You turn and run to catch up with the others. You climb the hill to Bethany, and you hear the disciples' anxious questions: "When will the temple be destroyed? How will we know when you are coming back?"

Dinner is a solemn affair. The disciples are feeling shocked at the day's events. And they don't know what to make of it.

You serve the meal tonight of grilled lamb chops with mint (you can substitute pork if you wish) and a side of tomato salad. Combine olive oil, red wine vinegar, honey, and red pepper flakes into a blend of olives, tomatoes, celery, and mint for your salad. Grill the chops with mint oil and sea salt. Top with sprigs of mint.

As you feast tonight with Jesus, let your mind wander to the events of your day. What do you most value in your life? Whom do you accept? Do you do the things you say? You wonder. You catch Jesus' eye. He is smiling at you. He nods. "You understand," he says.

Prayer

Lord, make me a servant of your kingdom. Keep my heart aligned with you. Amen.

24 Days to Resurrection

BREAKFAST: A SEASON FOR FIGS

"What more can I do for my vineyard?"

Jesus rises once again early in the morning. The people will already be gathering in the Temple waiting to hear him speak.

He comes to the table, and you offer him some warm figs spread with goat cheese, yogurt with honey, and sprinkled granola on top. To roast your figs, split them in half and preheat your oven to 400 degrees. Toss the figs with thyme, red wine, honey, and brown sugar. Add a bit of lemon juice and some balsamic glaze, and roast covered in foil for 30 minutes. Spread with goat cheese and allow to melt over the top. You can also sprinkle them with candied walnuts. Savor with a side of mango or coconut water and hot coffee.

Jesus points out to you that when the fig tree blooms, you will know that summer is near. For every time is a season. And the season of the Lord will come. No one will know when. For now, the tree is barren, as much of the world has become spiritually barren. But you, my disciples, will continue to invest in the kingdom, to put your faith and time into serving in my vineyard, keeping the covenant, finding your identity in me, and passing it on to others. The trustworthy servants will till and keep the covenant of the Master. In some that trust may be misplaced. But in those who have invested well and have continued to cultivate the Lord's garden-life in this world, nourishing in love, seeding in faith, giving others the gift of relationship with me, for the Father and I are one—they will see the glory of God's kingdom.

"Your Master will come on a day when you do not expect him and at an hour you are not ready for. So keep watch. Tend your heart. Till your relationship with the Father. Keep your roots firmly planted in me. I will be with you. Even if you don't see me, I will be with you always."

Prayer

Lord, help me to be like the fig tree that blooms, a disciple that comes of age in you. Nourish me each day in your love and grace and help me be aware always of your presence in every part of my life. Amen.

LUNCH

Jesus teaches in the Temple again all morning, and this time he keeps going through lunch, taking time only for a bowl of lentil soup, made with fresh lentils, spinach, vegetable broth, sautéed onions, cumin, cloves, cilantro, and some lime juice. You bring it to him in a clay bowl as he steps out of the Temple doors and into the courtyard. He looks around, as though seeing the world for the last time.

The palm and olive trees are swaying in the breeze. The sun feels warm on your back, and it bakes the clay soil of the streets. Children gather around Jesus, and he hands them the bread he brought from Bethany. It will be the last leavened bread for the next week. Today at sundown, the Holy High Feast will begin. The children sit at Jesus' feet, eating happily.

The sounds of the city reveal preparations for the Feast of Unleavened Bread that will begin at sundown. You can smell the baking bread and the rich spices that will make up the *karpas* (parsley dipped in salt water) and *charoses* (walnuts/wine/cinnamon/apples). The smell of horseradish that will make up the *chazeret* and bitter herbs (lettuce with horseradish) overpowers the steam from the roasting of eggs (*beitzah*) to be dipped in the salt water. The shank bone of the lamb (*zeroa*) from the *Korban Pesach* will be prepared today when the lambs are slaughtered. The preparations have been already going on. The Korban Pesach, the Temple Lamb, will be slain at precisely three p.m. The altar was prepared in the morning with oil, and the Lamb was tethered. Four cups of red wine will be used in the Seder meal. And merchants have been selling this and other bowls and pottery, candles, and cloths for the Pesach Festival for days. Now they put away their wares. The Feast will begin at dusk.

Before going back into the Temple to teach, Jesus calls to Peter and John, and he tells them to make preparations for the Passover meal. He sends them into the city to look for a man who has been alerted to reserve a place for them. Jesus tells them they will recognize the man because he will be the one carrying a large jug of water. Jesus says, "Follow him wherever he goes. He will go into a house. Follow him in and ask, 'Where is the room where the teacher can share the Passover seder with us, his disciples?' He will show you a second-story room with everything you need to prepare the meal." After the disciples leave, Jesus goes back into the Temple for his final afternoon. It will be the last time the people will hear him teach. They will meet in the evening for the celebration of Pesach.

Meanwhile, Judas has contacted the chief priests. They know they cannot arrest Jesus during the light of day during the festival. People would revolt. But Judas has an idea. They pay the disciple thirty pieces of silver to arrange for Jesus' betrayal that evening after the Passover meal is over. Judas knows Jesus will pray tonight. Once he knows where Jesus will be, he will go back and bring those designated by the priests and elders to arrest him—members of the *sicarii*, those who have been contracted to kidnap and bring Jesus to the chief priests and elders under the dead of night.

Jesus teaches until the time just before the feast is about to begin, when everyone will gather in their households to celebrate the Korban Pesach. Then Jesus leaves the Temple and makes his way to the house where the disciples were waiting.

Prayer

Lord, my heart is filled with sadness at what is to come, and yet with joy and reverence at the amazing sacrifice I know you have made. As I smell the cooking of the lamb, I realize the immensity of the sacrifice you have made for the sake of bringing humanity back into the arms of God. Help me, Lord, to be grateful each and every day for that sacrifice that has enabled my life. Amen.

SUPPER: THE FEAST OF PESACH-KIDDUSH AND THE NEW COVENANT SEALED WITH BLOOD

The Passover Feast will be your final feast with Jesus until the resurrection. From the time of his resurrection onward, he will feast with you always. But the next few days will be difficult and long. You feel your appetite waning.

The feast is a difficult one for all of the disciples. Jesus begins the feast by telling them it will be the last time he will eat Passover with them until all is fulfilled in heaven. He says this because the Feast will last for seven days, and the others will share additional meals. But this is the High Feast Day, and he will share the first matzo and cups of wine with all, along with the bitter herbs. Together, you will dip the parsley into the salt water, the symbol of the Lord's tears for all creation. According to the Jewish tradition, this night, you will recline to eat. The Passover ritual begins after the Kiddush with the washing of hands. Jesus says the blessing, the Kiddush, and leads you in the ritual of washing. But instead of washing your hands, he suddenly wraps a towel around his waist and stoops down to wash your feet instead.

You look around alarmed and confused as you feel him take your feet into his hands. You don't know what you should do. "What is the teacher doing?" you ask. The others look upset as well. Peter stands up and objects: "You will not wash my feet!" This upsets everyone very much because to wash someone's feet is not done, except by the lowliest of servants. It is considered a terrible debasement. But Jesus says, "You don't understand now, but you will later. I need to do this. Peter, if I don't, you will not know me as you need to when the time comes. You need to experience what I am teaching you with your body as well as your spirit. This feast must become part of you. And I want to make sure you remember the truth of who I am and what it means truly to be part of God's kingdom."

At this, Jesus finishes washing each disciple's feet, allowing you to experience his hands upon you, him kneeling before you. He wipes them dry, and then he reclines at the table again to continue the Feast. The experience has unsettled you. Jesus proceeds with the Passover Seder. He dips the parsley into the bowl of salted water. All of you dip as well as you begin reciting the Seder Haggadah: "Blessed are you, O God, King of the Universe, Creator of the fruits of the earth." Jesus breaks the bread, the matzo, and distributes it. "Let all those who are hungry, come and eat." But then he adds, "This is my body, my body given for you. Do this to remember me." He says this because he wants you all to understand he will take the place this Passover of the Korban Pesach, the Paschal Lamb, the sacrifice of life that will atone for all humanity and lead them back to God. That this sacrifice will be the redemption for all people who will repent and return to the Lord. The Son has made the way so that all can live eternally in the truth.

Then Jesus lifts up the cup of wine. And after the ritual blessing, he adds too, "This cup, which is poured out for you, is the new covenant, made in my blood." He says this to remind them all that as God cut the covenant with blood at the time of Abraham, now this new covenant, the salvation act of God through the Son, will be completed through the shedding of his blood. All of them are even more startled now. It's clear: the Master really means to go to his death. As the ritual of the Passover meal concludes, you sing the Hymns, the Psalms of the Hallel, followed by the Great Hallel, Psalm 136: "His mercy endures forever." The room gets quiet and still for a moment, and they all look at each other, wondering what to say. Then Jesus begins to speak again: "Do you understand what I have done?" he asks, referring to the way he washed you, and the way he spoke of the new covenant that the Passover sacrifice through him will seal. He pauses. He can see the events of the evening have unsettled everyone. "You call me Teacher and Lord, and yes, that is who I am. So, if I, your Lord and Teacher, am washing your feet, then you should wash one another's feet. No servant is greater than the master. If your feet are clean, then every part of you is clean." Then he pauses again. "But one of you who dips with me will betray me."

Jesus' face has gone pale. He looks visibly upset, and you feel a chill run down your spine as you realize one of you has betrayed the Teacher, the Lord. Immediately, the disciples begin questioning each other. Peter turns to John: "Do you know who it is?" he asks. John whispers, his voice barely audible, "Lord, who is it?" Then Jesus lowers his head. When he raises it, he says, "It is the one to whom I will give this piece of bread when I have dipped it in the dish" (John 13:26). Then, after he dips the piece of bread, he gives it to Judas Iscariot. And Jesus says firmly, "Go and do what you are going to." Alarmed, Judas stands up quickly and backs away. He hurries to the entrance of the room. Everyone can hear his footsteps down the stairs. The door opens, and he quickly disappears into the night.

The others look around. What is Judas going to do? Is he to do something with the treasury? Jesus says no more about it. But he lets them know he will be resurrected on the day of the Feast of First Fruits, the Feast symbolizing spiritual wholeness and union between human-ity and God. He will fulfill not only the Passover but the Feast of First Fruits as well. For though the seed had to die in order to break forth in life, it will, as a result of that death, grow tall and bear fruit.

"The Son of Man, that First Fruit of a new generation of human-ity, must be betrayed," he says. And he tells them, "You cannot go where I am going now. So, I give you a new command. Love each other. Remember the ways that I have shown you, the way tonight that I have loved you, as a servant, and show your love for others in the same way. If you do that, you will truly be my followers."

Then the others begin talking among each other, assuring one another that they will be the greatest of disciples. Peter vows to Jesus that he would give his own life to save the Master! But Jesus looks at Peter sternly: "Really? Let me tell you something you will do. You will deny me three times even before the dawn of this next day!"

Then he says to all of you: "Listen. You have stood beside me faithfully. You will eat and drink at my table in my kingdom. Simon Peter, I have prayed often for you that your faith will hold firm and you may become a source of strength for your brothers here. You know what the prophet Zechariah says: 'I shall strike the shepherd, and the sheep of the flock will scatter.' Each of you will stumble and fall tonight from me. But I will be raised up again, and I will see you again and lift you up, so that you know how to continue without me."

The evening's events have made you tremble. But you are rooted by your Master's side. You cannot do otherwise. He leads all of you to the Garden of Gethsemane to pray. Exhausted from the evening, you feel your eyes grow heavy, and you drift off to sleep.

Prayer

Lord, let me wait with you in your sorrow. Let me be a part of your story, your covenant, your redemption. Amen.

24 Days to Resurrection

BEFORE THE HOUR
FOR BREAKFAST

You've been sleeping deeply, the events of the night overwhelming. Now, startled, you wake to hear Jesus speaking. It is early in the morning now. The garden is dark. "Get up!" he says. "We have to go." You can hear the sounds of voices coming from a distance. "What time is it?" you wonder. You follow Jesus across the Kidron Valley to a ravine. Beyond it is one of his favorite olive gardens, the Garden of Gethsemane, where he gathers all of you together, just as Judas appears with a large group of Roman soldiers and Temple officials, sent by the chief priests and Pharisees. They are holding weapons. Some of them hold large torches to see through the darkness. Peter tries to hold Jesus back, but he steps forward: "Who are you looking for?"

"Jesus of Nazareth," one of them answers loudly.

"I Am the One." he says.

He looks at Judas standing with them. It gets quiet. Judas Iscariot comes forward to kiss the Master's cheek. No one else moves.

Some of them seem alarmed. Jesus repeats, "I have told you, I Am the One. If you are looking for me, then let the others go free."

Suddenly, Peter breaks the silence. He lunges toward Malchus, one of the high priest's servants, and with his sword, he severs the man's right ear. Jesus halts him: "Peter! Put down your sword. I must not turn away the cup the Father has given for me to drink. My mission must be fulfilled. I have told you this. It is time." Jesus heals Malchus, restoring his ear to him.

Troubled, the Roman commander steps forward then and arrests Jesus, and they take him under the dark of the still early hours to a place in the official quarters of the Temple, where he is brought before Annas, the father-in-law of Caiaphas, the high priest, for a closed meeting. The large room is filled with officials of the Temple, members of the Sanhedrin, witnesses, and some members of the Roman guard. Peter waits in the doorway. One of the other disciples is granted access to the room because he has a relationship with the high priest. In the courtyard, servants and officers gather around a fire. It is cold in the early morning hours, and Peter tries to warm himself. You linger in the doorway of the gathering place to listen. Annas is asking Jesus questions. Jesus is saying, "I've spoken in public, where the world can hear, not in secret. Why are you interrogating me? Many know what I have taught. It's not a secret." You cringe as one of the officers strikes Jesus.

You back away, not sure what to do. Tears well in your eyes as several of the men holding Jesus begin to insult him, beat him, and rough him up. You can see the red of the dawn now rising up from the east.

By the fire, you can hear one of the servants saying to Peter, "You're one of his disciples, aren't you?" You gasp as you hear Peter reply, "No. I'm not."

The high priest's servant comes over and says, "You were in the garden with him, weren't you?" All of them are looking at Peter, but

Peter continues to deny his involvement in the events of the night. It is dawning now, and the roosters are beginning to crow. You see Peter's head jerk up. He pales. He backs away from the group and disappears around the corner of the Temple wall.

You find a few bits of matzo in your pockets from the evening before. This will be your only breakfast this day. You heat some coffee by the fire.

Prayer

Lord, strengthen my faith. When difficulties rear their head, when calamities strike, help me to stay rooted in you, loyal to God, sure in my faith. Amen.

THE HOURS AFTER THE NOONTIME MEAL

By the time Jesus was bound as a prisoner and sent into the high priest's chambers, to Caiaphas, it was mid-morning. The Sanhedrin had called an emergency meeting in order to interrogate Jesus. Right in front of them, he declared himself the Son of God. It was with this that they charged him. "So, you are the Son of God, then?" the Sanhedrin officials charged. "It's as you say," Jesus replied.

It was the afternoon already of the Passover Feast Day when Jesus was taken from Caiaphas and the Sanhedrin's court to the governor's palace under guard. The high feast meant that the public would not be around to see what the Sanhedrin was doing. (The feast had begun at sundown the prior day and would end that evening.) Because of this, the Jewish officials could not enter the palace. It was a defilement to enter a gentile place on a High Feast Day. So, Pilate, the governor, met them outside. Pilate told them they should judge the man themselves by Jewish law. He didn't understand why they had brought Jesus to him. He had not broken any Roman laws. But the Jewish authorities insisted. They knew it was the only way to have the death penalty assessed. So, Pilate had Jesus follow him into the palace for questioning. When he realized Jesus was a Galilean, he knew he could pass the buck. This was not his jurisdiction. So, Pilate had Jesus sent over to Herod, who was visiting Jerusalem for the Feast. He would let him handle it.

Herod was nervous to meet Jesus because he had heard about him. (Herod had Jewish roots and had executed Jesus' cousin John.) He spent the rest of the day trying to talk to Jesus, but Jesus wouldn't answer his questions. Meanwhile, the chief priests, scholars, and others involved in the plot had followed and were angrily hurling accusations at Jesus from below. Finally, Herod got tired of Jesus and, insulted by his silence, he allowed his soldiers to mess him up a bit to show a bit of power. Herod mocked him, but still Jesus wouldn't answer. Eventually that night, tired of all of it, he dressed Jesus in robes fit for a king and sent him back to Pilate as a joke. Herod wanted nothing more to do with it. He didn't need another death torturing his conscience.

You desperately try to follow the crowd, to hear what is going on. Moving amidst the crowd, you manage to grasp some matzo and cheese around noon when Jesus is still with the Sanhedrin, along with some cups of water, Living Water, that you will keep with you as long as you possibly can.

Prayer

Lord, my stomach feels tied up in knots. The stresses of the day are upon me. Give me your peace. Help me trust in the knowledge that what is to pass this day and in my life will end with your victory. Amen.

THE EVENING IN DARKNESS AND FASTING

A long night of waiting and torture await the Master, your rabbi and teacher. You are waiting too, hoping that Pilate will let him go. You can tell he doesn't want to keep him. But he doesn't know what to do. The Temple Pharisees and high priests are pushing hard on Pilate. If they let him go now, who knows what Jesus will do? They want to see it through.

It's evening again when Pilate questions Jesus, but it is useless. He can see when he questions him that Jesus' mission among the people has nothing to do with a desire to usurp Roman power. He speaks of truth. This is a Jewish issue. It is the end of the High Feast Passover, and the time when Pilate will release one of his prisoners to the Jewish Sanhedrin. So, Pilate goes back out to the Jewish officials. "Look," he says, "I have nothing to charge this man with. You know that each year on the day of the Festival of Unleavened Bread I release one prisoner to you in honor of the Passover. Why don't I just release this man right now?"

"No!" The Temple authorities are determined to have their plan go through. Otherwise, they may never have another chance. One of them thinks of a response. "Give us Barabbas!"

Barabbas is an insurrectionist, a terrorist. Pilate is shocked. But the Temple powers that be will not relent. Pilate sighs and gives in. He orders Barabbas released. After that, he gives Jesus to the soldiers to be flogged and tortured. But he makes clear to the raging crowd,

"This is on you. I find this man innocent, and I want that to be clear. This is not my doing."

The chief priests and officers shout as the soldiers present Jesus, already flogged and beset with thorns and a mock robe, to the crowd of Temple officials. They are feeling powerful now that Jesus has no people around him. "Crucify him!" they yell. They shout, "He claims to be the Son of God. Our law says he needs to be put to death for sedition—blasphemy (heresy against the faith)!" By now it is late into the night.

Pilate, usually a calm man, is clearly jarred by the viciousness and determination of the Jewish authorities to have one of their own teachers executed. He brings Jesus back into his chambers again and tries to talk to him. But Jesus will not help Pilate to release him. "Don't you realize I'm trying to help you?" Pilate exclaims. He doesn't want to be responsible for the unwarranted death of this man. Jesus replies, "The one who handed me to you is guilty of the greater sin."

While he was questioning him, Pilate's wife had woken up and asked to speak with Pilate. She told him that she had dreamt about this Jesus, and she begged Pilate to have nothing to do with him.

It is the early hours of the morning now on Friday. The preparation day for the weekly Sabbath will soon begin. Spooked by his wife's strange dream, Pilate once more tries to release Jesus, but the Jewish authorities become angry and insistent, pressuring Pilate, saying if he releases Jesus, he will be betraying Caesar. Pilate is afraid and isn't sure what to do. He has a pitcher of water brought to him, and in front of the Sanhedrin, he washes his hands, letting them know that this act will be upon them. He will not take responsibility for Jesus' death. The Sanhedrin tells him, "It will be upon us then! Sentence him!"

At last, fearing the viciousness of the crowd, Pilate takes Jesus to the judgment chamber and officially renders judgment on him. It is six a.m. on the preparation day, and the city is just waking, when

Pilate hands Jesus over to the governor's soldiers to prepare for crucifixion. The Pharisees and Sanhedrin have successfully pulled off their plan. The people who so loved Jesus will find out too late when they wake that their beloved "Messiah" has been sent to Golgotha. Your heart is in your shoes, and you find it hard to eat tonight. You drink a thin soup and pray.

Prayer

Lord, hear my prayers. As Jesus prayed in the Garden of Gethsemane, before he was sent to be killed, hear my prayers. I ask you for many things in my life, Lord, but I trust you. Let my life be aligned with yours. Let your will be done. Amen.

24 Days to Resurrection

BREAKFAST ON THE DAY OF PREPARATION FOR THE WEEKLY SABBATH

Early in the morning, they forced Jesus and others to walk the road to Golgotha.

There he was hung in the morning sun.

Those who had plotted for his death looked on smugly, satisfied, feeling they had won.

Those who had followed him hung back in the distance, frightened, weeping in silence, and confused. Most did not yet know what had occurred because the chief priests and Pharisees had completed their task quickly and under cover of night in the midst of the festival day.

You too hang back from where the Temple officials and soldiers are standing. Hidden within the branches of an olive tree, you can see the pain on Jesus' face—as well as the quiet strength, the confidence, the strange calm.

You are shivering from the events of the last few days. This morning, you had only some coffee as you climbed the hillside to Golgotha and watched helplessly. The pit of your stomach is in turmoil. Your hands have gone cold with grief.

Yet you watch his face and cannot turn away. You must not turn away.

In him still, you find your security, and your faith endures. He looks up for a moment, and you could swear he is looking at you, reassuring you, even from the cross, where he is dying. You bring your hands to your face. He is nodding at you. With tears in your eyes, you nod back. Nothing will keep you from staying rooted in this place. You know God is with you, even here. Even now.

Prayer

Lord, in the hour of my most turbulent doubts, within the darkest of nights, I feel you. You stay with me. I will stay with you. Amen.

NOONTIME BLACKNESS

At noon, the sky grows black. The clouds seem to come almost out of nowhere. The atmosphere feels pregnant with signs of an impending storm. The air grows cool and the light casts an eerie glow over the hillside and the trees through the thickening clouds. The earth seems to steam with the change in pressure as wisps of fog form over the olive trees. And those around the crosses start murmuring. The earth feels strange. Some hang back or retreat to lower ground. Others are silent, watching.

And then in a powerful yet wavering voice, still wracked with pain, the sound of singing breaks into the stillness, echoing strangely in the fog. A chill passes through your body. It's Jesus. He is singing. You hear the *Ayelet Ha-Shachar*—Psalm 22, the messianic psalm of strength and salvation. You begin shaking uncontrollably, not from the cool of the morning but from the haunting words of the psalm, almost word for word recounting the chilling events of his death. You can see some of the Pharisees grow pale when they hear their own deeds called out within the psalm. The air has gone quiet, and one of the soldiers begins to back away, visibly upset. Jesus' voice endures through to the end of the song, this last song, growing agitated and excited at the end. Some of the soldiers and officials are looking frightened now. They've never experienced anything like this.

At the end of the psalm, Jesus almost shouts the final phrase, the victory call. Your body weakens and you fall onto your knees, as Jesus' hoarse yet determined voice shouts out, mustering all of the power in his weakened body: "All who sleep in the earth will rise up and bow down before God. All who have gone down into the dust will kneel in homage. And I will *live* for the *Lord!* My descendants will serve you! All generations to come will be told of the Lord. And they will proclaim his great mercy and righteousness to a people yet unborn, the redemption and deliverance he has brought—for *he has done it!*" In the circumference around the cross, all across the hill of Golgotha, you hear a gasp as the breath heaves forth from Jesus' body. In quiet whispering words, he says, "Into your hands, Father, I my spirit!" And then . . . he is still.

Suddenly, the earth begins to tremble underneath you. Still kneeling beneath the tree, you grip the ground as it quakes violently. You hear the gasps and screams of some of those near to the site. One of the soldiers, a centurion, is backing away, as though he's seen a ghost. He's trembling uncontrollably. Terrified, he turns and looks at the others. His face is white. His head is shaking. His eyes are wide with fear as he realizes what they've done. "He *was* the Son of God!" he falters. And he drops to his knees in terror.

You hear someone running and shouting: "The Temple! The curtain of the holy of holies has torn in two!" There is chaos now on Golgotha. It's just after three p.m., not much time until the Sabbath will begin. One of the guards says to another, "We need to get this done with. Go and break the others' legs." He reaches up and drives his sword into Jesus' side, releasing blood and water that come streaming down his side. They are taking down the crosses now. You can't watch any longer. You see Jesus' family still standing on the far side of the hill. You turn and find solace in the garden next to Golgotha, where you try to calm your spirit.

The day has passed. There will be no lunchtime today.

Prayer

Lord, sustain me even in this hour of need. Help me to wait for your still voice, the power of your resurrection. Amen.

SUPPER: MOURNING AND FASTING

"A time to weep and a time to laugh, a time to mourn and a time to dance ..." (Ecclesiastes 3:4).

"I will build you up again. ... Again you will take up your timbrels and go out to dance with the joyful. ... I will turn their mourning into gladness; I will give them comfort and joy instead of sorrow" (Jeremiah 31:4, 13).

At sundown, the weekly Sabbath will begin. Just before evening, after the crosses have been taken down, one of Jesus' secret disciples, Joseph from Arimathea, arrives on Golgotha hill. He went to Pilate to request the body of Jesus, and Pilate assented. Joseph prepares the body with linen wrappings sealed with a paste of myrrh and aloe oils, a preservative, and lays Jesus in his own tomb, which had been carved out of one of the rocks in the garden nearby. When he finishes the burial, he rolls a boulder over the opening of the cache-like tomb to seal it.

Still sitting on a rock amidst the olive trees, you watch Mary and Mary Magdalene. They are seated closer to the tomb. They watch Joseph perform the burial rites, but they remain after he leaves to console each other in silence. They mourn as they sit shiva with the dead. They will prepare to mourn for seven days, quoting Amos the prophet, "And I will turn your feasts into mourning" (Amos 8:10 KJV). You remember with them. You can't get Psalm 22 out of your mind. You remember the power in Jesus' voice. The women are gone now, and a gentle breeze whispers through the olive leaves. You hear their rustling, smell the sweet scent of myrrh still in the air. You remember then the words of the old familiar hymn, "Earth Has Detained Me Prisoner Long":

I would begin the music here ... and so my soul shall rise.
You turned my wailing into dancing; you removed my sackcloth and
clothed me with joy. (Psalm 30:11).

You rise slowly and go to join the others.

Prayer

Lord, my heart sings with the knowledge of your presence. I can feel you though I cannot see you. My faith esteems you. The eyes of my soul love you, and my ears hear and know your voice. You whisper to me in the wind. And I feel your rising. Amen.

24 Days to Resurrection

BREAKFAST ON THE SABBATH MORNING

This morning, you will eat a simple breakfast of matzo with honey, cinnamon, and blackberry preserves, along with scrambled eggs and coffee. It is still the week of the Festival, and all foods must be kosher. You prepare the coffee, as you have in the days up to Jesus' death. All of the Master's closest disciples are gathered around the table at Lazarus' house with you, recalling what occurred the day before at Golgotha.

As you pray together, a messenger arrives with news. He tells Simon Peter that the chief priests and Pharisees went early this morning to see Pilate and requested that guards secure the tomb and keep watch, in case any of Jesus' disciples might try to steal his body and then claim he had been resurrected. They said, "If that happens, then we would have been better off just leaving him alive!"

He says that Pilate gave them permission to secure the gravesite. He also reports that Joseph, a member of the council from Arimathea, offered the resting place hewn in the rock of his own accord. Joseph was a good man, a disciple, and he objected to the Council's actions. Jesus still had friends in the Sanhedrin, those who remembered and cherished the days when the Great Hillel ruled the Sanhedrin with a gentle hand, along with his vice president, Menahem the Essene. Those days are long gone. Now the Shammai rule with an iron fist and blood on their hands. And those who object to the Eighteen Measures, the strictly imposed purity laws, or the Shammai's underhanded politics and powerplays, do so in secret.

The disciples return to the table in prayer. It is the weekly Sabbath, and nothing more will happen today. Tomorrow will be the Feast of First Fruits. They can discuss what to do after the Festival is over. As the household prepares to celebrate the Sabbath, you decide to take a walk in the olive garden where Jesus spent so much time when he was with you. There, you pray.

Prayer

Lord, what do I do now without you? How do I know what is before me, or which way I should go? Lead me, Lord. Give me direction. Help me to put my trust in you, and in the others who mourn you with me. We are your body now. Teach us how to stay rooted in you. Amen.

NOONTIME WATCHING AND WAITING

When you arrive back at the house, you see several of Jesus' disciples looking troubled. No one has prepared the noontime meal. The air is thick and quiet. You ask Matthew, who is near the doorway, what happened. "Judas is dead," he replies. Matthew continues: I think Judas acted impulsively. He was angry, and he only wanted to stop the Master from doing some of the things he thought he shouldn't. He never thought he would be convicted and sent to be killed by his own colleagues. He apparently tried to go and give the money back. He said, "I can't keep this money! I've done wrong! I've betrayed an innocent man! His blood will be on my hands!" He had hoped perhaps he could still save Jesus in time, that the temple authorities would listen to him when he said Jesus was innocent. But the chief priests sent him away and wanted nothing to do with him now that they had what they wanted. They only used him to get to Jesus.

> "When Judas realized the kind of men they were, he couldn't face what he had done. And the council wouldn't take back the money. They said, 'The state of your soul is none of our affair. Go on your way!' Judas apparently was beside himself with grief and guilt, and he threw down the money right there in the Temple. Then he went off and hanged himself." (Matthew 27:3-5 Author's paraphrase)

The disciples looked visibly upset. They know how wily the Temple Shammai can be. Judas was duped by them. But he was also overtaken by his own anger, greed, and self-righteousness. Later, he was plagued by guilt, as well. He couldn't bear the thought that he had been responsible for the death of his Master and Teacher, and a rabbi! And he had been his disciple. Jesus had trusted Judas. So many had wanted Jesus dead. But they hadn't been able to touch him. The Master had been betrayed in the end by one of his own, one of his beloved students, a leader from the closest circle of his disciples.

You wonder about your own life. How many times have you betrayed him in your heart, in one way or another? You feel grief not just for the Master, but for Judas as well. You know if the Master were here, he would lay his hands on Judas and let him know he was forgiven. Why couldn't Judas have faith in the mercy of the anointed one? If only Jesus were here. He would know what to do.

Prayer

Lord, I am troubled by the reality of sin and guilt, the kind that tears away at the heart and strips the soul of its faith. Lord, I need your forgiving and healing hand, lest I tremble and fall away. Let me never doubt the depth of your mercy, Lord. Or the lengths to which your love will go. Amen.

THE EVENING SABBATH ENDS / THE FEAST OF FIRST FRUITS BEGINS

The table this evening is filled with discussion of the events of the week. You dine with the others on parsnips, matzo, and eggplant. Onions, eggplant, tomatoes, and mushrooms are seasoned and mixed with matzah farfel, then baked at 400 for 30 minutes. The parsnips are baked in olive oil and seasoned with cilantro.

It is the seventeenth day of the month of Nisan, and at sundown, the Feast of First Fruits will begin. As evening approaches, the people of Jerusalem are bringing in the first sheaves of barley from the fields for the ritual to celebrate the first day of the harvest.

"The grain that you sow has to die and be broken before it comes forth in a new life." You remember the words that Jesus spoke: "I must die to be glorified." *Could it be?* you wonder.

As stipulated in Leviticus, new life begins the day after the seventh Sabbath that falls after the Passover Feast, on the first day of the week, on the day of the Feast of First Fruits. You think of the way Jesus spoke to you about his resurrection, the way he explained it through the metaphor of the seed.

Leaving the others behind, you start running down the hill toward the Mount of Olives. You are running so fast that you are out of breath, but you don't care. You reach the edge of Jerusalem and turn toward the hill of Golgotha. Then, pausing only for a moment, your breath coming in heaves, you start up the hill to the garden.

"But Christ has indeed been raised from the dead, the first fruits of those who have fallen asleep" (1 Corinthians 15:20).

Prayer

Lord, I feel the joy heaving in my heart, the praise bursting from my soul. Laughter springs from my chest, and I know the Lord my God is Lord of Life. Lord of All. Amen.

24 Days to Resurrection

THE FEAST AT DAWNING

Somewhere, a stick crackles. The air is thick with the dew of dawn when you wake. The scent of the garden around you reminds you where you are. You rise up quickly to see two women coming up the path toward the rock. You hurry to join them. They nod at you, and you go with them.

As you approach, the light becomes blinding white, and you must duck under the branches of a nearby olive tree to see. The woman have gone into the open tomb looking for Jesus. They come out confused. You feel your face go warm.

"It's true," you whisper.

Then you see him. All three of you at once. He is walking among the trees. He turns to you and greets you. You know his voice.

You fall onto your knees. Mary cries out, "Rabboni!"

You watch as he speaks with them. Then he looks at you. He smiles and nods.

You get up. He motions for you to follow the women. You don't hesitate this time.

You know he will go before you.

Your heart sings. The sun is coming up over the trees, and the whole world looks different to you today.

He is risen.

You go and prepare for the Feast.

χαῖρε!

My Lenten
Journal

Lenten Study Calendar

YEAR:

ASH WEDNESDAY:

BIBLE STUDY MEETING TIMES:

MAUNDY THURSDAY:

GOOD FRIDAY:

THE DAY OF RESURRECTION:

SCAN HERE to learn more about
Invite Ministries—created to invite people to a deeper
faith and living relationship with Jesus Christ

www.ingramcontent.com/pod-product-compliance
Lightning Source LLC
Chambersburg PA
CBHW020243130626
46549CB00005B/2044